UNIVARIATE TIME-SERIES ANALYSIS OF QUARTERLY EARNINGS: SOME UNRESOLVED ISSUES

by

William S. Hopwood

Florida State University

and

James C. McKeown

University of Illinois at Urbana-Champaign

AMERICAN ACCOUNTING ASSOCIATION

1986

Library of Congress Catalog Card Number 85-062985
ISBN 0-86539-059-2
Printed in the United States of America

UNIVARIATE TIME-SERIES ANALYSIS OF QUARTERLY EARNINGS: SOME UNRESOLVED ISSUES

AMERICAN ACCOUNTING ASSOCIATION

The By-Laws of the American Accounting Association state that the first purpose of the Association shall be "to initiate, encourage, and sponsor research in accounting and to publish or aid in the publication of the results of research." In harmony with this objective, the publication of the Studies in Accounting Research is aimed at encouraging and publishing research. This series is an outgrowth of the research program initiated by the Association in 1965. Under this program research projects and authors are selected by the Director of Research, who is assisted by a Research Advisory Committee.

When the project is commissioned, the author is allowed maximum freedom in conducting research. The author is solely responsible for the procedures followed and the research conclusions.

This project was commissioned by A. Rashad Abdel-khalik during his term as Director of Research. It was completed when William R. Kinney, Jr. was Director of Research. The Research Advisory Committee for this project consisted of:

William Collins	University of Oklahoma
Bala Dharan	Rice University
Paul Griffin	University of California-Davis
Kenneth Janson	Michigan Technological University

TABLE OF CONTENTS

PREFACE

The authors wish to express their gratitude to A. Rashad Abdel-khalik, Theodore J. Mock, and William R. Kinney, Jr., Directors of Research of the American Accounting Association during this study's progress from proposal to completion. We received many constructive comments from their advisory committees and particularly the Project Advisory committee, Professors William Collins, Bala Dharan, Paul Griffin, and Kenneth Janson. In addition, we have benefited from the comments of our colleagues at the University of Illinois at Urbana-Champaign and The Florida State University, and the participants in presentations at the University of Colorado, Purdue University, and the Third International Symposium on Forecasting where portions of this project were presented and vigorously discussed.

Financial support for the conduct of this study was provided by the American Accounting Association, Caterpillar Tractor Company, and Coopers and Lybrand. The authors, of course, accept full responsibility for the contents of the monograph.

William S. Hopwood
James C. McKeown
Champaign, Illinois
May, 1985

CHAPTER ONE

Time-Series Research in Accounting

In recent years there has been a rapid growth of time-series research in accounting. This has led to applications in several areas including those of auditing, financial reporting, and management accounting. These applications have provided insight into the stochastic properties of key variables (e.g., sales, income, and security price returns) within the accounting environment. Yet, at the same time, they have raised a large number of substantive and methodological issues. This monograph focuses on some of what we consider important unresolved issues relating to univariate time-series research in accounting. Throughout, the primary emphasis is on the time-series properties of accounting earnings per share since this has been the area of the largest quantity of research activity. Furthermore, the Financial Accounting Standards Board (FASB) has stated, "The primary focus of financial reporting is information about earnings and its components" [FASB, 1978, p. ix].

The specific set of unresolved issues dealt with in the present research includes:

(a) Problems relating to the stationarity and invertibility of estimated autoregressive integrated moving average (ARIMA) model parameters (Chapter Two).

(b) Investigating the benefits derived from the use of power transformations in ARIMA models (Chapter Three). The ARIMA models, popularized by Box and Jenkins[1] [1976], represent a broad class of time-series models that have been used in many accounting research studies.

(c) A technique to identify intervention models without dividing the earnings series into two parts, since sufficiently long time-series typically are not available for splitting a series into shorter subseries (Chapter Four).

(d) Investigating the impact of selecting the appropriate differencing and trend specifications for ARIMA models (Chapter Five).

(e) Investigating the private value of advance knowledge of future quarterly earnings. For example, could one obtain private value, in the present quarter, from advance knowledge (i.e., a perfect forecast) of a company's quarterly earnings four quarters in the future (Chapter Six)?

The issues dealt with in this research were selected on the basis of being (1) primarily methodological in nature, and (2) directly or indirectly referred to in previous research. However, the issues are not necessarily strongly related to each other, nor do they constitute an exhaustive list of issues meeting the criteria above. They are, however, issues that we have seen appear on a recurring basis in the accounting literature (as discussed in subsequent chapters). The first four issues relate primarily to problems with model choice and assumptions. These four issues all can be viewed as directly or indirectly relating to the appropriate choice of the functional form of the model or the

---

[1] This seminal work is now in its second edition, but was first published in 1970.

violation of one or more assumptions. The fifth issue deals with the choice of the forecast horizon in an informational content context. This choice, like the appropriate model form, must be made by the researcher. Since all five issues involve methodological choices confronting the user of time-series analysis in accounting, we believe that knowledge gained in the univariate setting concerning these issues will provide an important foundation as accounting research moves into the use of multivariate time-series and other complex methodologies.

The present study provides a quick review of the literature for individuals not completely familiar with previous studies. This review is given in the remainder of the chapter along with a description of the population used for the research. Subsequent chapters address and expound upon the issues listed above. The last chapter summarizes all of our findings and deals with implications for future research.

Readers not familiar with the ARIMA class of models and the Box-Jenkins time-series methodology might benefit from reading Nelson [1973] before reading the remainder of the monograph. The study is admittedly technical in nature; however, each chapter has a reasonably nontechnical summary for those interested primarily in the essence of our findings.

A Brief Review of Time-Series Research in Accounting (TSRA)

The purpose of this section is to provide a brief survey of some of the major applications of time-series research in accounting (for a detailed survey, see Abdel-khalik and Thompson [1977-78], Hopwood and Newbold [1981], and Bao, et al. [1983]). Subsequent chapters build on the discussion presented here.

Factors Motivating TSRA

Since accounting is concerned with providing information for making decisions, and decisions in the business environment involve the use of (explicit or implicit) forecasts, it is not surprising that accounting is concerned with time-series.[2] For example, Norby [1973] found that a large percentage of financial analysts use earnings forecasts in their decision-making process. In addition, Penman [1980] found that ''insider'' information relating to annual corporate earnings forecasts would enable an investor to earn ''abnormally'' high returns (as measured by the capital asset pricing model of Sharpe [1964], Lintner [1965], and Mossin [1966]). Such a possibility has led the Securities and Exchange Commission to favor the concept of urging and/or requiring the disclosure of earnings forecasts. (For a detailed discussion, see Gonedes [1976], Penman [1980], Prakash and Rappaport [1974], and the *Wall Street Journal* [1978].) Their reasoning in part has been that, in the name of fairness, all potential investors should have equal access to the best forecast available, especially in the case where the forecast is based on inside information.

[2] By time-series analysis, we refer to statistical model building that treats variables as processes that evolve over time according to some sort of regularity. The regularity, of course, is never perfectly clear to the researcher because of randomness in the data. One important use of time-series models is in extrapolation or forecasting.

The use of forecasts by investors has been recognized in the accounting literature. For example, Beaver, et al. [1968] considered "predictability" as a possible criterion for assessing the usefulness of alternative reported financial numbers. Under this view, different numbers can be compared on the basis of how well they can be used to predict some variable of interest.

The Financial Accounting Standards Board [1976, p. 55] has stated:

> Earnings from an enterprise for a period measured by accrual accounting are generally considered to be the most relevant indicator of relative success or failure of the earnings process of an enterprise in bringing in needed cash.

From this statement it can be seen that the "variable of interest" has been considered, at least by the Financial Accounting Standards Board, to be some form or measure of enterprise cash flow. More debatable, however, is the notion of using past earnings to predict future earnings. While this type of approach has been operationalized (see, for example, Frank [1969] and Simmons and Gray [1969]), Revsine [1971] has argued convincingly that forecasted earnings is not of interest in its own right. It is only interesting if it can be used to aid in prediction of other variables or outcomes.

Another motivating factor for TSRA has been information content/capital market research. In testing the informational content of accounting numbers, researchers have hypothesized that the capital market reacts to new or "unexpected" information about a particular company. This requires the computation of an expectation or prediction of the accounting number. The predicted number is then subtracted from the actual and the difference (both sign and magnitude) is then hypothesized to convey either "good" or "bad" news to the market. If this hypothesis is correct, then the difference will be associated with abnormal returns as defined by the capital asset pricing model of Sharpe [1964], Lintner [1965], and Mossin [1966]. This methodology was introduced by Ball and Brown [1968] and has been applied by many, including Brown and Kennelly [1972], Foster [1977], and Joy, et al. [1977]. The results of this body of research have consistently shown that the market reacts to both the sign and magnitude of unexpected earnings, thus supporting (though not proving) the hypothesis that accounting earnings information is, in fact, used by investors. For example, Foster [1977] used an autoregressive model (a particular type of time-series model) on the seasonal difference of quarterly earnings to generate a prediction of earnings. (This model is described in detail at a later point in the monograph.) The prediction error from this forecast was found to be associated with abnormal returns as discussed above.

TSRA has also been applied to analysis of security returns. Fama [1965, 1970] showed that under certain conditions such returns should be white noise (i.e., serially uncorrelated) if prices reflect all past market information. Therefore, Praetz [1979] used spectral analysis to test for a flat spectrum. In addition, his white noise hypothesis was tested by Lookabill and McKeown [1976] by correlogram analysis. The results of these studies tend to be consistent with the hypothesis that prices do, in fact, reflect *all* past market information, thus indicating that an individual investor cannot gain any advantage over other market participants by use of past market data alone.

An additional application of TSRA is in the analytical review phase in auditing. As part of the audit, the accountant must conduct substantive tests to assess the reliability of account balances. In part, these tests include "analytical review of significant ratios and trends and resulting investigation of unusual fluctuations and questionable items'' [Stringer, 1975, p. 15]. This has motivated researchers (e.g., Kinney [1978] and Albrecht and McKeown [1977]) to employ time-series techniques for forecasting of account balances. Actual balances can be compared to forecasted balances, and large differences can be considered for detailed investigation. This technique has the potential for being developed to the stage where it becomes of general use to auditors.

In summary, a number of factors have contributed to the motivation of TSRA. It should be pointed out that the above discussion is not meant to be comprehensive, and other undiscussed areas of application exist. Foster [1977] discusses some of these, including research relating to cost of capital, dividend policy, and income smoothing. These issues are not discussed here since they have received relatively less attention relating to time-series analysis in the accounting literature.

Research Findings

As discussed above, the primary focus of this study is on the research use of time-series analysis of accounting earnings. The high quantity of research activity in this area has been motivated in part by the primary focus of financial reporting on earnings and its components. The discussion that follows in the remainder of this chapter thus is limited to the time-series analysis of earnings and its components.

Central to TSRA has been an attempt to find a model or models that adequately describe the earnings process. Little attention in the accounting literature has been devoted to the time-series properties of the components of earnings. This can at least partially be attributed to the fact that only very recently has any consensus (see Collins and Hopwood [1980]) about the nature of the underlying earnings process itself begun to emerge. In addition, the study of earnings components, since it involves more than one time-series, tends to lend itself to multivariate time-series analysis, a field that is still in its infancy within accounting.[3] Early studies dealing with the time-series properties of earnings used simple naive and/or index models due to the lack of tools to identify and estimate more sophisticated models. These include Little [1962], Green [1964], Little and Rayner [1966], Green and Segall [1967], Ball and Brown [1968], Cragg and Malkiel [1968], Beaver [1970], Brown and Kennelly [1972], Coates [1972], Copeland and Marioni [1972], and Reilly, et al. [1972]. These studies used simple ''rule of thumb'' models such as the average of previous values. Later, Dopuch and Watts [1972], Ball and Watts [1972], and others introduced the Box-Jenkins [1976] modeling technique into the accounting literature and focused on the time-series behavior of annual earnings. Watts [1975], Foster [1977], Griffin [1977], Brown and Rozeff [1979], Collins and Hopwood [1980], Hopwood and McKeown [1981], and others, applying the same methods, focused on the stochastic behavior of quarterly earnings. The findings of these studies are discussed below.

---

[3]Reasons for the slow development of multivariate time-series in accounting include both methodological and data constraints. The methodology is relatively new, and low-cost, easy to use multiple time-series programs are not yet widely available. In addition, traditional data sources such as the Quarterly Industrial COMPUSTAT tapes do not contain complete, consistent data for many variables beyond earnings.

The results of the annual earnings studies provide a substantial amount of evidence that annual earnings or earnings per share follow a random walk with drift or a random walk.[4] Support for this conclusion comes from Little and Rayner [1966], Brealey[1969], Beaver [1970], Ball and Watts [1972], Lookabill [1976], and Salamon and Smith [1977]. In addition, Albrecht, et al. [1977] and Watts and Leftwich [1977] found that full Box-Jenkins analysis of individual series did not provide more accurate forecasts than those of the random walk or random walk with drift. Therefore, their results did not provide evidence to reject the hypothesis that the use of this single or "premier" model is the most appropriate procedure, at least in the cases studied.

Research on quarterly earnings has also involved a consideration of a premier versus individual series model approach. Several univariate premier models have been investigated in the past. These include those of (using the notation of Box and Jenkins[1976]):

(a) Foster [1977], who considered the $(1,0,0) \times (0,1,0)_4$ model

$$(1-\phi B)(1-B^4)X_t = a_t + C$$

(b) Griffin [1977] and Watts [1975], who considered the $(0,1,1) \times (0,1,1)_4$ model

$$(1-B)(1-B^4)X_t = (1-\theta B)(1-\theta_4 B^4)a_t$$

(c) Brown and Rozeff [1979], who considered the $(1,0,0) \times (0,1,1)_4$ model

$$(1-\phi B)(1-B^4)X_t = (1-\theta_4 B^4)a_t$$

where $B^k X_t \equiv X_{t-k}$.

Note that the Foster model is a special case of the Brown and Rozeff model with $\theta_4 = 0$. (The Foster model also contains a constant, but Brown and Rozeff [1979] found this parameter not to be useful.)

Lorek [1979] and Collins and Hopwood [1980] explored the relative predictability of these three premier models and found that there was no advantage to performing individual series identification, at least for forecasting horizons within one year. Both of these studies focused on the ability of the models to generate annual forecasts from quarterly earnings. The method used involved summing the quarterly forecasts to produce an annual forecast. As the year progressed, realizations were substituted for forecasts in computing the annual sum.

More recently, researchers have begun to explore multiple time-series models. (While this topic is not directly applicable to this monograph, we include a short discussion for completeness.) For example, Hopwood and McKeown [1981] found that the model

$$(Y_t - Y_{t-4}) = W_0(X_t - X_{t-4}) + \frac{(1-\theta B^4)}{(1-\phi B)} a_t + C$$

---

[4] A random-walk-with-drift model for the series X_t is defined as:

$$X_t = X_{t-1} + \delta + a_t,$$

where δ is a drift term and

a_t is a serially uncorrelated error series.

The random-walk model is the special case of the random-walk-with-drift model above with the drift term (δ) equal to zero.

provided more accurate forecasts than those of the univariate models discussed in the preceding paragraph in predicting annual earnings from quarterly earnings. In this model, Y_t denotes quarterly earnings per share and X_t a forecasted market index of quarterly accounting earnings.

Also Beaver, et al. [1980] developed a time-series model that predicted annual earnings more accurately than the random walk model by using security prices as a lead indicator. Similarly, Chant [1980] found forecast improvement by using the money supply as a single leading indicator of earnings. In summary, these studies have expanded the information set used to predict earnings.

Population of Firms Included in Study

In order to provide a stable basis for this study, each segment of the study will use the same basic group of firms.[5] The group of firms studied will be all firms which meet the following criteria:

(a) Their fiscal year ended on December 31 throughout the period 1962-1978.

(b) Their quarterly primary earnings per share (EPS) were available on the COMPUSTAT quarterly industrial tape for the entire period.

(c) They were listed on the New York Stock Exchange with no missing monthly returns from 1970 through 1978.

Since these 267 firms include all firms which meet the criteria, we are studying all firms to which the results could be generalized. We will, therefore, refer to this group as a population. Also, the results observed are population parameters. As such, any statistics which might normally be inferential are actually provided as additional descriptive statistics to aid the reader in interpreting the results.

Summary

This chapter has defined the scope of the remainder of this monograph. It has also briefly summarized previous research and outlined the population to be studied.

[5] The Chapter Six population is actually a subset of this group of firms as described on page 39.

CHAPTER TWO

Problems Relating to Stationarity and Invertibility Conditions for ARIMA Models

As discussed below, certain restrictions must apply to an ARIMA model (defined below) in order for it to be valid. Furthermore, some "canned" programs allow violation of these restrictions without warning. Given this, we conducted a rough survey of ARIMA models published in previous papers within *The Accounting Review* and *Journal of Accounting Research*. In most of those studies which tabled some or all of their models, we found models with parameters which violated the restrictions.[1] In one study, about one-fourth of the tabled models were in violation.

Given the prevalence of the problem of these violations, the present chapter attempts to (1) measure the impact of the problem on forecast errors for quarterly earnings per share, and (2) investigate the potential benefits of constrained estimation, where the parameter estimates are constrained to lie within the appropriate valid region.

The Stationarity and Invertibility Region for the Model Parameters[2]

All autoregressive-moving-average time-series models can be written in the form [Box and Jenkins, 1976, p. 95]:

$$(1)\quad Z_t = \phi_1 Z_{t-1} + \phi_2 Z_{t-2} + \dots + \phi_n Z_{t-n} - \theta_1 a_{t-1} - \theta_2 a_{t-2} - \dots - \theta_L a_{t-L} + a_t$$

where Z_t is the time-series variable of interest, a_t is the error term and $\{\phi_i, \theta_i\}$ represent the autoregressive and moving-average parameters, respectively.[3] This is known as the difference equation form of the model. Alternatively, the time-series model has an equivalent random-shock form [Box and Jenkins, 1976, p. 95]:

$$(2)\quad Z_t = a_t + \psi_1 a_{t-1} + \psi_2 a_{t-2} + \dots$$

or inverted form [Box and Jenkins, 1976, p. 101]:

$$(3)\quad Z_t = a_t + \pi_1 Z_{t-1} + \pi_2 Z_{t-2} + \dots$$

Both represent an infinite series with (2) forming a weighted sum of present and past values of a "white noise" process a_t and (3) forming a weighted sum of previous values of Z_t, plus a random shock.

It is clear that either (2) or (3) will diverge to infinity unless certain restrictions are placed on the parameters of (1), namely the roots of

$$\text{(a)}\quad (1 - \phi_1 X - \phi_2 X^2 - \dots - \phi_m X^m) = 0$$

$$\text{and (b)}\quad (1 - \theta_1 X - \theta_2 X^2 - \dots - \theta_m X^m) = 0$$

---

[1] Upon written request, the authors will provide a list of such studies.

[2] The reason for the terminology "stationarity and invertibility" is complex and not discussed in this paper. The interested reader should consult Chapter 3 of Box and Jenkins [1976].

[3] In practice, Z_t might be a differenced series (i.e., a series of changes). Also, a constant term can be included in the model.

must have absolute values greater than one.[4] Restriction (a) is typically referred to as the stationarity condition and restriction (b) is referred to as the invertibility condition. The reasonableness of these restrictions can be seen from examining the following first-order autoregressive model:

$$Z_t = \phi_1 Z_{t-1} + a_t, \qquad \phi_1 = 1.1.$$

Here the restriction is that the root of

$$(1 - 1.1X) = 0$$

must be greater than one. This is clearly violated in this case since the root can be found by setting 1.1X equal to one and solving for X, which equals 1/1.1 or .909. In general, the root for this model is $\frac{1}{|\phi_1|}$ and the stationarity restriction is satisfied when $|\phi_1| < 1$. Consider the effect on the forecast function when $|\phi_1|$ is greater than 1. In the above situation, the first forecast is $1.1Z_N$, where Z_N is the last observation in the observed series. The next forecast is $1.1\hat{Z}_{N+1}$ or 1.1^2Z_N. The next forecast is $1.1\hat{Z}_{N+2}$ or 1.1^3Z_N. Finally, the forecast for time N+k is 1.1^kZ_N. In other words, the last observation is effectively compounded at the rate of ten percent per period, resulting in explosive growth of the forecast function. This is clearly problematic because the estimation process of ϕ_1 assumes that the mean of the series is fixed over time.

An Example

Consider a hypothetical special case of the model proposed by Griffin [1977] and Watts [1975] for modeling quarterly earnings per share:

$$Z_t = (1 - .1182B)(1 - .31027B^4)a_t$$

where B is the lag or backshift operator such that $B^n a_t = a_{t-n}$. This model can be converted to the form (1) by expansion of its two factors by simple algebraic multiplication. This gives approximately

$$\begin{aligned} Z_t &= (1 - .1182B + (.1182B)(.31027B^4) - .31027B^4)a_t \\ &= (1 - .1182B + .0366749B^5 - .31027B^4)a_t \\ &= a_t - .1182a_{t-1} - .31027a_{t-4} - (-.036674a_{t-5}) \end{aligned}$$

Solving for the roots of:

$$1 - .1182X - .31027X^4 + .036674X^5 = 0$$

gives three real and two complex roots, namely

1) 8.46024, 2) -1.3399, 3) 1.3399i 4) -1.3399i and 5) 1.3399

Since the roots 1, 2, and 5 are real and have absolute values greater than one, and the norms of 3 and 4 are both equal to 1.3399 and are greater than one, the model meets the validity test for invertibility.

---

[4] In the complex case, each norm must exceed one [Box and Jenkins, 1976, p. 74]. The norm of a complex number is analogous to the absolute value of a real number since both represent a measure of distance from zero.

Application to a Population of Firms for Some Models Commonly Used in the Literature

From Chapter One, several models have been considered in the literature as useful representatives of the quarterly earnings per share process. These are (1) a consecutively and seasonally differenced first-order moving-average model [Griffin, 1977, and Watts, 1975], (2) a seasonally differenced first-order autoregressive model [Foster, 1977], and (3) a seasonally differenced first-order autoregressive and seasonal moving average model [Brown and Rozeff, 1978]. In Box and Jenkins' notation [1976, Chapter 9], these are designated as (0,1,1) x (0,1,1), (1,0,0) x (0,1,0), and (1,0,0) x (0,1,1), respectively, and will henceforth be referred to as the GW, F, and BR models. To demonstrate empirically the applicability of the root criterion, the above three models were estimated using primary EPS (earnings per share before extraordinary items) for a sample of 267 firms.[5] The models were estimated with 48 quarters of data beginning with the first quarter of 1962 and ending the last quarter of 1973. The models were reestimated 16 additional times with one new quarter of data added each time. Four forecasts (from one to four quarters ahead) were made with each estimated model.

Table 2-1 presents the mean absolute relative forecast error[6] for those models having at least one root whose norm is less than .88. Although any root with a norm less than one is a problem, norms near the borderline probably will not result in drastic deterioration of the prediction results. Thus, a cutoff somewhat below one was used. A lower cutoff would show more divergence; a higher cutoff, less divergence. As can be seen, the series with models whose roots have norms that fall below the cutoff perform worse than series with norms above the cutoff in comparison to individually identified (and valid) Box-Jenkins (BJ) models for the same series.[7] This is the case even for the short forecast horizons used here. Note the general pattern of increasing difference as forecast horizon increases for both BR and F.

The statistical significance of the difference between these forecast errors was computed by testing the difference in the proportions of positive forecast error differences (where the individually identified BJ model forecast had smaller error than the BR

---

[5] As described in Chapter One, the firms met the following criteria:

a. Their fiscal year ended on December 31 throughout the period 1962-1978.

b. Their quarterly primary EPS were available on the COMPUSTAT quarterly industrial tape for the entire period.

c. They were listed on the New York Stock Exchange with no missing monthly returns from 1970 through 1978.

[6] In order to control for the possibly different difficulty of predicting different series, the numbers shown in Table 2-1 are the mean of absolute relative forecast error for the stated model minus the absolute relative forecast error of the forecast from an individually identified Box-Jenkins model for that same observation. Thus, negative numbers indicate the stated model had lower absolute relative error than the Box-Jenkins models for the same set of forecasts.

[7] See Box and Jenkins [1976] for a discussion of model identification techniques. Of the 4,539 individually identified models, 35 had the same form as BR, 66 same as F, and 14 same as GW. See Table 5-1 for numbers of models with the same "profile" (as defined in Chapter Five).

or F model). The specific null hypothesis tested was that the proportion of cases where the BJ model was better was not greater for the models whose root norms fell below the cutoff than for the models whose root norms were above the cutoff:

$$H_0\colon p_G \leq p_B$$

where:

p_G = proportion of cases where BJ model forecasts were more accurate than the forecasts from F or BR models whose root norms exceeded the cutoff; and

p_B = proportion of cases where BJ model forecasts were more accurate than the forecasts from F or BR models whose root norms fell below the cutoff.

This test was applied to each model and forecast horizon separately, with the results as shown in Table 2-1. Basically, for all horizons for both the BR and F models, the null hypothesis was rejected at the five percent level (with most of the rejections also supported at far lower alpha levels). This supports the statement that the BR and F models whose root norms fell below the cutoff provided inferior forecasts.

The GW model doesn't exhibit as much differentiation. Although the forecasts from the models below the cutoff are relatively poorer than the models above the cutoff, the differences are smaller, do not exhibit the pattern of increasing differences with greater forecast horizon, and generally are not statistically significant. Further investigation of this behavior led to the discovery that *all* 42 BR models which had roots below the cutoff had those ''invalid'' roots in equation (a) above related to the autoregressive parameter in the model. Similarly, *all* problems with the F model are in the same equation (a) since the F model contains no moving average parameters. This leads to the potential conclusion that violation of the stationarity root criterion in equation (a) is probably more likely to lead to deterioration of forecast accuracy than violation of the invertibility root criterion in equation (b).

Knowing that most researchers are not anxious to solve potentially complex equations, an analysis of ways of simplifying the validity testing was conducted. For the F and BR models, the root of equation (a) has a norm of $\frac{1}{|\phi_1|}$ where ϕ_1 is the autoregressive parameter. For the BR model, the root of equation (b) must also be considered, but that root is simply $\sqrt[4]{\left|\frac{1}{\theta_4}\right|}$ where θ_4 is the moving average parameter. Thus, for either of these models, any parameters with absolute value greater than one will lead to a violation of the root criterion. Unfortunately, solution of equation (b) for the GW model is not as simple (see Dharan [1983a]). Therefore, an attempt was made to find a more readily applied guideline. For this (fairly large) sample, it turns out that a simple rule of rejecting all GW models with either parameter having absolute value greater than 1.1 gives satisfactory discrimination on forecast accuracy. Thus, as shown in the last section of Table 2-1, it seems that this simple ''rule of thumb'' has some usefulness within the present context. We conclude by summarizing the rule of thumb as follows:

> Reject models which contain either autoregressive parameters larger than 1.1 or moving average parameters larger than 1.1.

Table 2-1

Demonstration of the Effect of Model Invalidity on Mean Absolute Relative Forecast Error*

			Number of quarters ahead forecasted				
			1	2	3	4	N
MODEL	BR	$p > .88$	-.0206	-.0154	-.0065	-.0105	4497
		$p < .88$	.0749[c]	.2504[a]	.3218[a]	.5087[b]	42
	F	$p > .88$	.0118	.0225	.0270	.0234	4517
		$p < .88$	.0874[c]	.2235[b]	.4822[a]	.6838[a]	22
	GW	$p > .88$	-.0059	.0067	.0223	.0247	4408
		$p < .88$	.0567	.0713	.0835	.0329	131
		$\theta < 1.1$	-.0054	.0063	.0198	.0214	4466
		$\theta > 1.1$	.0754	.1460	.2844[b]	.2434	73

$$^{*}\ \left|\frac{\text{Prediction} - \text{Actual}}{\text{Actual}}\right| - \left|\frac{\text{BJ Prediction} - \text{Actual}}{\text{Actual}}\right| \quad \text{(each truncated at 3.0)}$$

p = norm of minimum root of characteristic equation

θ = maximum moving average parameter value

Code for proportion of positive signs of forecast errors from "bad" models significantly greater than proportion of positive signs from "good" models:

Code	α level
a	$< .001$
b	$< .01$
c	$< .05$
[no code]	$> .05$ (not significant)

The next issue explored was the benefit of using constrained estimation, where the parameters were constrained to the valid region. We used a simple technique to accomplish this, namely the *penalty method* (see Luenberger [1973]). This involved adding a penalty to the objective function, during nonlinear least squares estimation, whenever a parameter became arbitrarily close to the appropriate boundary. Specifically, the following term was added to the sum of the squares during estimation:[8]

$$\begin{cases} |\beta + \delta - MR| * 10^{20} & , \text{ if } \beta + \delta > MR \\ 0 & , \text{ otherwise} \end{cases}$$

where β is the polynomial root boundary described above, MR is the minimum root of either characteristic equation, and δ is a small constant arbitrarily close to zero.

The above program modification is very simple to make, as there are many standard subroutines that are readily available which provide the required roots. The root-finding subroutines need to be called each time the sum of the squares is computed by the estimation routine. At this point, the above penalty is added if the smallest norm of any root is less than one. The nonlinear minimization process will therefore automatically avoid situations with out-of-bounds (invalid) parameters.

Table 2-2 essentially displays results for the cases in Table 2-1 where the parameters were out of bounds. For example, note in Table 2-1 that there were 42 such cases for the BR model and 22 for the F model. In Table 2-2, these same cases are presented, but the numbers reported represent the differences in forecast accuracy between the constrained and unconstrained models. In each case, a positive number indicates that constrained estimation produced an improvement in forecast accuracy.

Note that for the BR model the difference ranges from 12.04 percent at one quarter ahead to 54.84 percent at four quarters ahead, in the case where the minimum root is equal to or less than .88. The same result is also true for the GW model, but the differences are of smaller magnitude, ranging from approximately two to three and one-half percent. Also, when a cutoff value of one is used as a root criterion, the BR model shows improvement in the approximate range of one to eight percent. A cutoff of one, however, produced little or no benefit in the case of the GW model. The results for the cutoff of one as compared to the cutoff of .88 indicate that greater margins of violation of the root criterion cause greater deterioration of forecast accuracy.

The statistical significance of the differences shown in Table 2-2 was computed by testing the null hypothesis that the proportion of cases where the bounded model forecast was more accurate than the unbounded model forecast was not greater than .5, or:

H_0: $p \leq .5$

where:

p = proportion of cases where the bounded model forecasts were more accurate than the forecasts from the unbounded models whose root norms exceeded the cutoff.

---

[8] We wrote our own program to perform the constrained estimation using penalty and barrier methods suggested by Luenberger [1973]. The authors will provide details on request. The procedure is very simple to apply and therefore is essentially cost-free.

Table 2-2

Difference in Mean Absolute Relative Forecast Error*
Attributable to Bounded Estimation

			Number of quarters ahead forecasted				
			1	2	3	4	N
MODEL	BR	$p < .88$	.1204[a]	.3282[a]	.4213[a]	.5484[a]	42
		$p < 1.0$	.0178[a]	.0667[a]	.0754[a]	.0857[b]	430
	F	$p < .88$	.0873[a]	.2235[a]	.4822[a]	.6838[a]	22
		$p < 1.0$	.1063[a]	.1701[a]	.3576[a]	.4018[a]	95
	GW	$p < .88$	.0194	.0118	.0207	.0351	131
		$p < 1.0$	.0076	-.0043	.0022	.0022	898
		$\theta > 1.1$	-.0141[b]	.0747	.1415	.1437	73

$$^{*}\left|\frac{\text{Prediction (non-bounded)} - \text{Actual}}{\text{Actual}}\right| - \left|\frac{\text{BJ Prediction (bounded)} - \text{Actual}}{\text{Actual}}\right|$$

(each truncated at 3)

p = norm of minimum root of characteristic equation

θ = maximum moving average parameter value

Code for proportion of cases where forecast error of bounded model less than forecast error of unbounded model significantly greater than .5:

Code	α level
a	$< .001$
b	$< .01$
c	$< .05$
[no code]	$> .05$ (not significant)

This test was applied to each model and forecast horizon separately, with the results (shown in Table 2-2) that the bounded F and BR models had significantly superior forecasting ability, but the differences for the GW models were generally not significant.

One additional factor discovered in this section of the research deserves mention. Even though the GW models whose root norms fell below the cutoff (or whose parameters were greater than the criterion) did not show significantly more cases where their forecasts were inferior, the proportion of forecast errors which had to be truncated (at the chosen limit of three) was generally greater for all horizons for all models at all cutoffs. This reemphasizes the point that the biggest danger of using models which have invalid parameters (i.e., whose roots fall outside the appropriate valid region) is that since the models have no expectation function, the forecasts generated by these models will have unknown properties. While a forecaster using these models may get away with it some of the time, there will be cases where the forecasts will be very bad.

Summary

Overall, the results of this chapter indicate that in a reasonable number of cases, the sample roots of the BR and GW models fall out of bounds. In addition, substantial improvements in forecast accuracy for the BR and F models were achieved in the cases where constrained estimation was used, especially in the case where the minimum root was less than .88.

One should not attempt to generalize the numerical quantities observed in this study to other populations or samples. The problem, by its very nature, is unpredictable. This is because models with out-of-bounds parameters produce nonsensical parameter estimates and forecasts. In addition, our experience has shown that the estimation process can become very unstable when the parameter estimates cross a boundary. Stated differently, it is already well known that models with invalid parameters should not be used. The present study simply documents the occurrence of the problem with quarterly EPS, and implements and tests a simple correction technique.

CHAPTER THREE

Power Transformations

Graphical analysis of quarterly earnings per share (for our 267-firm population) suggests a variance increasing over time. A common approach for dealing with this problem is to select a transformation such that the time-series X_t follows an ARIMA process with a constant variance after being transformed. One class of transformations that has been particularly useful in the literature is the one introduced by Box and Cox [1964]:

$$X_t^{(\lambda)} = (X^{\lambda} - 1), \qquad \text{if } (\lambda \neq 0)$$
$$X_t^{(\lambda)} = \log (X_t), \qquad \text{if } (\lambda = 0)$$

where λ is estimated simultaneously with all other model coefficients (we shall refer to this estimated value as $\hat{\lambda}$). While the Box-Cox transformation was originally introduced for problems relating to linear regression and analysis of variance, Hopwood, McKeown, and Newbold [1981] (henceforth HMN) found that it improved forecast accuracy for BR and GW and individually identified (BJ) models.

In their study, they considered four possible transformation strategies:

(a) use a Box-Cox transformation with λ simultaneously estimated with the other model parameters;

(b) use the logarithmic transformation;

(c) use no transformation; or

(d) use a decision rule based on a 95-percent confidence interval for $\hat{\lambda}$. If this interval contains $\lambda = 1$ but not $\lambda = 0$, use no transformation. If the interval contains $\lambda = 0$ but not $\lambda = 1$, use the logarithmic transformation. If the interval contains neither $\lambda = 1$ nor $\lambda = 0$, use $\hat{\lambda}$. If the interval contains both $\lambda = 0$ and $\lambda = 1$, use whichever is closer to λ.

The last strategy is motivated by a point stressed by Box and Cox [1964], namely that if possible, the transformation should make physical sense. For economic data, this suggests a strategy that tends to favor either no transformation ($\lambda = 1$) or the logarithmic transformation ($\lambda = 0$). The latter makes sense because, as Nelson [1973, p. 53] argues, economic data often increase at an approximately constant percentage rate (which causes an increasing variance). Furthermore, he proves in this situation that a logarithmic transformation with differencing will produce a constant variance in the transformed series.

Hopwood, McKeown, and Newbold [1981] found that strategies (c) and (d) dominated strategy (a). In addition, (b) resulted in forecast errors larger than in the case of no transformation at all. Their analysis involved a random sample of 50 firms, with 84 observations being used in each case for statistical estimation. In the current work, we apply a similar analysis to our 267-firm population (described in Chapter Two), and use 17 different base periods to obtain a broader result. An additional advantage of the population as used in the present study is that it involves the use of shorter base periods (48 to 64 observations) than those in the HMN study (84 observations). This is important because the length of the series might have an impact on the desirability of a transformation since longer series might display more pronounced effects of increases in variability.

Finally, it should be emphasized that the class of transformations studied in the present research deals with what is known in the econometric literature as "functional-form analysis." (See, for example, Judge, et al. [1980].) This type of analysis focuses on using the time-series (and estimation) process to determine the most appropriate functional form for the model. Other types of transformation, such as deflation by a price-level index, might also be used. In the present study, we focus on the Box-Cox transformation class because it was originally introduced into the literature for purposes of normalizing residuals.

A related objective of the present research is to investigate the distributional properties of the model residuals. There has been little or no research in accounting that has studied the sample residual distributions of ARIMA models for earnings. Therefore, this study analyzes these distributions for normality, both before and after transformation. Our study looks at:

(a) Sample skewness

(b) Sample kurtosis

(c) V_2/V_1

where V_2 is the variance for the second half of the series, and V_1 is the variance for the first half of the series.

Empirical Results

For each of the 267 series, the BR, GW, and F models were estimated (using each of the above four transformation strategies) for 17 base periods, with the first estimation interval containing 48 observations, the second estimation interval containing 49 observations, etc.[1] In each case, forecasts were computed for a one- to four-quarter forecast horizon.[2] Forecast error metrics were computed based on mean absolute relative error [MARE = average of: |(actual-predicted)/predicted|], mean squared relative error [MSRE = average of: $((\text{actual-predicted})/\text{predicted})^2$] and mean rank. Tables 3-1, 3-2, and 3-3 present these computations for the BR, GW, and F models, with the forecast errors averaged across all of the base periods. In addition, to eliminate the potential problem of near zero denominators in the MARE and MSRE metrics, errors larger than 3.0 were truncated to 3.0. We explored a wide range of truncation values and found that the choice of a particular value did not change our overall results.

Note that the data in Table 3-1 are fairly consistent across the various error metrics. In each case, the log is a poor strategy. Second, the decision rule produced errors slightly

---

[1] We considered the possibility that the transformation might change the identification of the premier models. Detailed analysis indicated that this was not the case.

[2] For series where the transformed models produced forecasts which could not be inverted, an untransformed or logged model was used depending on whether $\hat{\lambda}$ was closer to one or zero. These cases were eliminated from the comparison of forecast errors (because they were not actually based on transformed data).

TABLE 3-1

Prediction Results for Transformation Comparison (BR Model)

METRIC/Data Transformation	HORIZON			
	1	2	3	4
MEAN ABSOLUTE RELATIVE ERROR				
Estimated Lambda	.27098	.32585	.35256	.36317
Log	.33643	.38778	.40655	.41312
Untransformed	.27526	.33147	.35826	.36861
Rule	.28255	.33783	.36339	.37216
MEAN SQUARED RELATIVE ERROR				
Estimated Lambda	.26911	.35957	.40144	.42869
Log	.43459	.53547	.57668	.59505
Untransformed	.27383	.36452	.40951	.43168
Rule	.28842	.38811	.43083	.45290
MEAN RANK				
Estimated Lambda	2.42066	2.47841	2.50645	2.52523
Log	2.62686	2.54976	2.47939	2.44435
Untransformed	2.44575	2.48696	2.53434	2.55257
Rule	2.50673	2.48486	2.47981	2.47785

This analysis includes base periods 48 through 64.

Truncation Value for Relative Error = 3.00

	HORIZON			
	1	2	3	4
PROPORTION TRUNCATED				
Estimated Lambda	.01093	.01654	.01934	.02243
Log	.02439	.03112	.03336	.03448
Untransformed	.01065	.01654	.02019	.02131
Rule	.01149	.01794	.01990	.02243

larger than in the untransformed case. Also, the estimated lambda strategy produced errors slightly smaller than in the untransformed case, but only in the neighborhood of one-half of one percent for the one and four quarters ahead forecast horizons. Given that these differences are small and that there is uncertainty due to slight differences in the frequency of truncations across strategies as well as nonindependence across time horizons, strategies, and firms, it is not possible to conclude in favor of using the power

TABLE 3-2

Prediction Results for Transformation Comparison (GW Model)

METRIC/Data Transformation	HORIZON			
	1	2	3	4
MEAN ABSOLUTE RELATIVE ERROR				
Estimated Lambda	.27943	.34331	.37502	.39044
Log	.37722	.45268	.49293	.51436
Untransformed	.27952	.33786	.36491	.37383
Rule	.29505	.36028	.39521	.41310
MEAN SQUARED RELATIVE ERROR				
Estimated Lambda	.28627	.41330	.46871	.50267
Log	.47949	.64653	.73501	.79230
Untransformed	.29032	.39989	.44345	.46497
Rule	.30780	.44122	.50497	.54775
MEAN RANK				
Estimated Lambda	2.33122	2.36723	2.35851	2.37398
Log	2.80534	2.79578	2.79325	2.78678
Untransformed	2.33727	2.32124	2.32855	2.32377
Rule	2.52616	2.51575	2.51969	2.51547

This analysis includes base periods 48 through 64.

Truncation Value for Relative Error = 3.00

	HORIZON			
	1	2	3	4
PROPORTION TRUNCATED				
Estimated Lambda	.01097	.02053	.02335	.02504
Log	.02335	.03404	.03882	.04473
Untransformed	.01294	.01800	.02110	.02138
Rule	.01125	.02082	.02363	.02560

transformations with the current data.[3] Additional support for this line of reasoning comes from the results in Tables 3-2 and 3-3, where the differences were usually small and not consistently in the direction favoring the estimated lambda strategy.

[3]This finding differs from that of Hopwood, McKeown, and Newbold [1981]. This difference can be accounted for by differences in sampling restrictions as previously discussed.

TABLE 3-3

Prediction Results for Transformation Comparison (F Model)

METRIC/Data Transformation	HORIZON			
	1	2	3	4
MEAN ABSOLUTE RELATIVE ERROR				
Estimated Lambda	.28189	.34024	.36437	.37278
Log	.39542	.44871	.46883	.47365
Untransformed	.27949	.33774	.36393	.37275
Rule	.29719	.35599	.37813	.38428
MEAN SQUARED RELATIVE ERROR				
Estimated Lambda	.28408	.38789	.43831	.45390
Log	.54806	.65817	.71411	.73418
Untransformed	.27993	.38260	.43399	.45119
Rule	.30802	.42098	.47101	.48402
MEAN RANK				
Estimated Lambda	2.36958	2.38904	2.38462	2.37902
Log	2.71500	2.65429	2.61362	2.57678
Untransformed	2.40421	2.45844	2.53301	2.57663
Rule	2.51120	2.49823	2.46876	2.46758

This analysis includes base periods 48 through 64.

Truncation Value for Relative Error = 3.00

	HORIZON			
	1	2	3	4
PROPORTION TRUNCATED				
Estimated Lambda	.01297	.01886	.02034	.02210
Log	.03212	.03772	.04067	.04126
Untransformed	.01149	.01798	.02210	.02269
Rule	.01267	.01857	.02181	.02358

Analysis of Residuals

To our knowledge, no previous studies in accounting have presented detailed analyses of residuals generated from estimated time-series models for quarterly earnings per share. In the present section, we conduct such an analysis, on both a before- and after-transformation basis.

TABLE 3-4

Residual Statistics

		Box-Pierce Q Statistic	Skew*	Kurtosis*	Variance Ratio	Res Sig 1	Res Sig 2
Untransformed	BR	11.453	–.275	3.669	8.833	.065	.850
	GW	10.299	–.227	3.525	8.540	.069	.825
Log	BR	9.169	–.895	4.562	33.153	.049	.302
	GW	7.943	–.872	4.325	32.032	.048	.294
Estimated λ	BR	10.624	.108	–.079	2.307	.015	.134
	GW	9.142	.119	–.113	2.257	.009	.130

Key: Variance Ratio ≡(variance of second half) / (variance of first half)

Res Sig 1 — average number of residuals, per series, in the first half that exceed three standard deviations in absolute value.

Res Sig 2 — average number of residuals, per series, in the second half that exceed three standard deviations in absolute value.

*Skew and kurtosis would be zero for a normally distributed population.

Table 3-4 gives several statistics for the BR and GW models, assuming the log, estimated lambda, and no-transformation strategies. These include the Box-Pierce Q statistic, sample skew, and sample kurtosis. In addition, the last two columns contain the average number of residuals, per firm, that exceed three standard deviations. The sample skew is computed as:

$$\text{sample skew} \quad \frac{m_3}{m_2^{\ 3/2}}$$

where m_2 and m_3 are the second and third sample moments respectively, computed as:

$$m_i = \frac{\Sigma(X-\overline{X})^i}{n-1} \ .$$

The sample kurtosis is computed as:

$$\text{sample kurtosis} = (m_4/m_2^2) - 3.$$

Both sample skew and kurtosis have expected values of zero for normal distributions and large sample standard deviations of $\sqrt{6/N}$ and $\sqrt{24/N}$, respectively (subsequently used for testing purposes).

The Box-Pierce statistics of Table 3-4 are consistent with all of the models having adequate fit on average, with no significant average residual autocorrelation.[4] The skew

[4] Some researchers use an improved version of the Box-Pierce statistic. See Box and Ljung [1976].

statistics are also consistent with normality, since the critical value for an individual series for a sample size in the range of 50-60 is approximately .5 in absolute value at an alpha level of five percent. The exception is the log which actually induces significant negative skew that does not appear in the untransformed case. Note that the log also produces a marked degradation of the other statistics when compared to the untransformed case. On the other hand, the kurtosis, variance ratio, and residual outlier statistics all indicate a marked improvement for the transformed series. For example, the BR average kurtosis is 3.6699 before transformation and -.079 afterwards. Since the critical value for an individual series is about .8, the pretransformed average exceeds the critical value, but the transformed average does not. The variance ratio statistics, however, indicate that the variance of the second half of the series is, on average, in excess of twice the magnitude of the variance of the first half, even after transformation. In addition, the average number of outliers in the second half is in excess of ten times of the average number in the first half. This indicates that the transformation does not produce a constant variance over time. Note, however, that the transformation substantially reduces the increasing variance problem, since the variance ratio exceeds a value of 8.0 without transformation.

Summary

In summary, for the 17-year period studied (1962-1978), the kurtosis statistics of the untransformed model residuals indicate a marked departure from normality. The variance ratio indicates a severe problem with a variance increasing over time. In general, the log transformation made things worse, but the Box-Cox transformation resulted in converting the distributions to a nonkurtotic state. Also, the Box-Cox transformation improved, but did not completely eliminate, the problem of increasing variances.

Finally, even though the transformation produced substantial improvement in the residual distributions, the forecasts from the transformed models were not superior to those of untransformed models. This indicates a need for either a different transformation technique or longer time-series (since the transformed series produced more accurate forecasts for the longer time-series used in Hopwood, McKeown, and Newbold [1981]). Another approach might be to consider a more general nonlinear time-series model or a Kalman filter model [Jazwinski, 1970] that allows the variance to change over time.

CHAPTER FOUR

The Problem of Intervention Analysis With Small Samples

Researchers within accounting and finance have devoted a considerable amount of effort to studying the time-series properties of corporate income. However, few of the published papers in this area have considered the impact of intervening events on their data. The problem is complicated because intervening events can make the model identification process difficult. Box and Tiao [1975], in recognizing this problem, suggested that only data prior to (or after) the intervention be used for model identification. In this way, the sample correlations are not "contaminated," and presumably a better identification is made. Unfortunately, this approach is not always feasible since one might not have enough data to divide the series in two. This is particularly true with quarterly or annual accounting data where, at most, 25 years of data are typically available.[1] Therefore, this chapter explores a technique that allows intervention-noise model identification without splitting the series into two parts.

Complete Data Intervention-Noise Model Identification

Box and Tiao have suggested that univariate time-series with single intervening elements be represented by models of the form:

$$y_t = \frac{W(B)}{\delta(B)} \xi_t + \frac{\theta(B)}{\phi(B)} a_t, \qquad (1)$$

where $W(B)/\delta(B)$ represents the transfer function on ξ_t, a dummy parameter equal to either zero or one, depending on the occurrence of an exogenous event. Also, y_t represents the stationary univariate time series of interest, and $\frac{\theta(B)}{\phi(B)}$ is the noise model for the white noise series a_t. Note that with the transfer function deleted (or when ξ_t is always 0), (1) reduces to an ARIMA model for y_t.

The difficulty is that the noise model in (1) may not be identifiable from the autocorrelations of the y_t series. One standard technique used to handle this problem in single-input transfer function analysis is to make a preliminary estimation of (1) with the impulse response weights estimated in place of the transfer function, while $\frac{\theta(B)}{\phi(B)}$ is taken to be one. In the present situation, the residual series from this estimation, called the noise series, denoted by $\hat{N}_t = y_t - \frac{\hat{W}(B)}{\hat{\delta}(B)} \xi_t$, would then be the y_t series "ad-

[1] Even where more than 25 years of data can be gathered, the assumption of the same underlying process over the entire period is often quite tenuous. Therefore, this problem tends to preclude longer time-series, even if additional data are available.

justed'' for the exogenous events. Take, for example, the simple situation:

$$y_t = W_0\xi_t + \frac{\theta(B)}{\phi(B)} a_t,$$

where $\xi_t = 1$ for $t = t_0$ and zero otherwise. Assume, without loss of generality, that y_t (for $t \neq t_0$) has a mean of zero; then this procedure would minimize $\Sigma(y_t - W_0\xi_t)^2$ and yield an estimate of W_0 equal to y_{t_0}. This would produce a corresponding noise-series value equal to zero at $t = t_0$. Note that while zero might be the unconditional mean of the noise series, it might differ considerably from the conditional expectation of N_t given that the noise model $\frac{\theta(B)}{\phi(B)}$ is simultaneously estimated with W_0. It is, therefore, possible in a given situation that failure to incorporate information in the noise series might lead to an estimate of W_0 sufficiently poor so as to lead to an incorrect identification of the noise model. An obvious way to solve this problem might be to estimate the noise model simultaneously with the transfer function, but this is not possible since at this stage, the noise series is unknown.

One way to solve this problem might be to obtain a preliminary estimate of W_0 by simultaneously estimating it with a high-order autoregressive approximation for the noise model. The resulting estimated W_0 then would be used to generate a noise series which then could be used to identify the noise model.

A summary of the application of our procedure to the above hypothetical situation is:

(a) create an ''adjusted'' series which is the original time-series with the impact of the intervening event removed. This is done by approximating the unknown model for the series with a high-order autoregression while fitting a dummy parameter to the observation for which an intervention exists;

(b) identify a model for the ''adjusted'' series;

(c) simultaneously estimate the parameters for the model in (2) with the parameter for the dummy variable; and

(d) perform the usual diagnostic-model modification steps.

Note that for the above hypothetical situation, $\delta(B)$ and $W(B)$ from equation (1) are assumed to be one and W_0, respectively. Our method, of course, is equally valid for an arbitrary choice of these two terms. The choice of these terms should depend on the nature of the intervening event and its impact on the series. In general, events that are immediately assimilated into the series are consistent with $\delta(B)$ being equal to one. This effectively eliminates this term from the model. On the other hand, if a ''shock'' to a series is assimilated over a prolonged time period, the output lag term ($\delta(B)$) is not unity. This can be seen by examining the transfer function portion of the model in equation (1), namely

$$y_t = \frac{W(B)}{\delta(B)} \xi_t.$$

This can also be written as

$$y_t = W(B) \cdot \frac{1}{\delta(B)} \xi_t.$$

Here, the term $\frac{1}{\delta(B)}$ is an infinite series in the backshift operator B. This series is

$$1 + \psi_1 B + \psi_2 B^2 + \psi_3 B^3 + \cdots$$

For example, if $\delta(B)$ is assumed to be $(1\text{-}\delta_1 B)$, then the power series equivalent is

$$1 + \delta_1 B + \delta_1^2 B^2 + \delta_1^3 B^3 + \cdots,$$

which, as well known in mathematics, converges to $\frac{1}{1\text{-}\delta B}$, assuming $|\delta| < 1$.

It is very important to note that the structure of the $\delta(B)$ and $W(B)$ part of the model depends on the nature of the intervention at hand. One must have knowledge of the underlying event. It would be inappropriate to use an intervention term without knowing that some event has occurred. The fact that a plot of a series reveals an observation that appears discordant is not sufficient justification to use intervention analysis. However, one might investigate such discordant observations to find that some intervening event has in fact occurred. For example, a plot of sales might reveal that one value appears very low and completely inconsistent with the pattern otherwise observed. A follow-up investigation might reveal that some kind of catastrophe such as a warehouse fire occurred. In this case, an intervention model would be appropriate. If no extraordinary event occurred, then the technique should not be applied.

A main reason for not applying intervention analysis when it is not called for is loss of information. The likelihood function for the model parameter estimates is heavily influenced by the squared deviations of the fitted versus actual values. This means that discordant observations will have a relatively large influence on the parameter estimate because of the squaring of the deviations. That is, each observation is essentially weighted according to the square of its deviation. Therefore, in this context, discordant observations contain the "most" information. Intervention analysis essentially assumes that the discordant event does not provide information about the process, but rather about the exogenous event in question.

Two Accounting Earnings Series

Table 4-1 presents quarterly earnings per share (EPS) (adjusted for changes in capital structure) for Bethlehem Steel (BS, 116 quarters) and Maytag (48 quarters). Note that BS has a very large loss of $10.92 at observation 107, and Maytag has losses of $.03 and $.19 at observations 37 and 38. Analysis of the corporate section of the *Wall Street Journal Index* revealed that the BS loss was caused by a combination of work stoppages and plant closings. Also, a large portion of the Maytag losses can be attributed to a five-month strike. Both cases are analyzed on an individual basis.

Table 4-2 shows the sample autocorrelations (ACs) and partial autocorrelations (PCs)

TABLE 4-1

Bethlehem Steel Company								
Quarters	**Quarterly Earnings Per Share**							
1- 8	.62	.58	.44	.98	.45	.10	.40	1.25
9- 16	.77	.70	.85	1.01	.69	.76	.63	1.22
17- 24	.88	1.18	1.01	1.45	1.13	1.26	.07	1.37
25- 32	1.16	1.09	.86	1.02	.52	.61	.55	1.23
33- 40	1.06	1.59	−.90	.69	1.10	.62	.24	.56
41- 48	.14	.53	.71	1.16	.81	.46	.27	.26
49- 56	.39	.61	.35	.76	.59	.85	.76	.91
57- 64	.96	.98	.70	.62	.80	1.18	1.01	.73
65- 72	.70	.74	.50	.90	.95	1.09	.48	1.03
73- 80	.75	.94	.81	1.06	.65	.59	.33	.48
81- 88	.74	1.08	.15	1.17	.56	.83	.46	1.17
89- 96	.91	1.32	1.29	1.20	.99	1.60	2.47	2.79
97-104	1.84	1.14	.83	1.73	.65	1.25	1.04	.91
105-112	−.58	.80	−10.92	.43	.02	1.95	1.48	1.70
113-116	1.36	2.36	1.71	.88				

Maytag Company								
Quarters	**Quarterly Earnings Per Share**							
1- 8	.26	.21	.25	.25	.29	.25	.24	.29
9- 16	.33	.27	.33	.29	.31	.26	.27	.30
17- 24	.29	.25	.31	.35	.27	.28	.31	.42
25- 32	.39	.28	.39	.51	.37	.33	.40	.52
33- 40	.39	.36	.41	.54	−.03	−.19	.54	.58
41- 48	.47	.42	.54	.66	.50	.44	.62	.64

for the BS series. Note that both ACs and PCs are small relative to their sample standard errors at lags one and four, thus indicating a near-white noise process. Following our procedure described above, we fitted the following model:

$$y_t = \hat{W}_0 \xi_{1,t} + C + \frac{a_t}{(1-\hat{\phi}_1 B-\hat{\phi}_2 B_2-\hat{\phi}_3 B_3-\hat{\phi}_4 B^4)}, \qquad (2)$$

with $\xi_{1,t} = 1$ for $t = 107$, and zero otherwise.

This produced an initial estimate of W_0 equal to -11.52 with a standard error of .41. Note that this estimate is similar in magnitude to the earnings in the quarter with the large loss of $10.92. In other words, this gives an "adjusted" value to the series equal to $.60

TABLE 4-2

BS Series: Sample Statistics for Original Series

Lag	Autocorrelation		Partial Autocorrelation	
	Coefficient	Standard Error	Coefficient	Standard Error
1	.0954	.0928	.0954	.0933
2	.2042	.0937	.1968	.0937
3	−.0598	.0974	−.0989	.0941
4	−.0010	.0978	−.0292	.0945
5	−.0925	.0978	−.0610	.0949
6	−.0034	.0985	.0116	.0953
7	−.1722	.0985	−.1523	.0958
8	−.0531	.1011	−.0401	.0962
9	−.0688	.1013	.0019	.0967
10	−.0794	.1017	−.0898	.0971
11	−.1543	.1023	−.1520	.0976
12	−.0906	.1042	−.0702	.0981

TABLE 4-3

BS Series: Sample Statistics for Noise Series Using High-Order Noise Model Approximation

Lag	Autocorrelation		Partial Autocorrelation	
	Coefficient	Standard Error	Coefficient	Standard Error
1	.3930	.0928	.3930	.0933
2	.3110	.1062	.1852	.0937
3	.1405	.1138	−.0390	.0941
4	.3026	.1153	.2580	.0945
5	.0888	.1219	−.1273	.0949
6	.1659	.1225	.0862	.0953
7	.0395	.1244	−.0392	.0958
8	.1330	.1245	.0380	.0962
9	−.0743	.1257	−.1440	.0967
10	.0528	.1261	.0660	.0971
11	−.0910	.1263	−.0985	.0976
12	.1209	.1269	.1638	.0981

TABLE 4-4

Maytag Series: Sample Statistics for Original Series

Lag	Autocorrelation		Partial Autocorrelation	
	Coefficient	Standard Error	Coefficient	Standard Error
1	.4392	.1443	.4392	.1459
2	–.0278	.1699	–.2735	.1474
3	.2025	.1700	.4528	.1491
4	.3579	.1750	.0102	.1508
5	.0886	.1896	–.0688	.1525
6	–.1574	.1905	–.1577	.1543
7	.0461	.1932	.1712	.1562
8	.2281	.1934	.0107	.1581
9	–.0619	.1989	–.1811	.1601
10	–.2704	.1993	–.0587	.1622
11	.0710	.2068	.2413	.1644
12	.2336	.2073	–.0688	.1667

(\$11.52 - \$10.92). This is the expected value of this observation, using all of the data, had the intervening event not occurred. The resulting residual series was white noise, thus indicating the usefulness of the high-order autoregressive approximation in the noise model.

The ACs and PCs from the noise series (i.e., "adjusted series" in (2)) are given in Table 4-3. Note that these statistics are quite different than those in Table 4-2. In this case, both seasonal and nonseasonal components are indicated. This means that simple univariate analysis of the autocorrelation of the unadjusted series would be highly misleading and result in an incorrect model identification. In this case, the intervening event completely masks the basic autocorrelation pattern. Therefore, we fitted an ARIMA $(1,0,0) \times (0,1,1)_4$ model to the noise series while simultaneously fitting the intervention parameter (with the difference being on the data series). This gave significant noise model parameters, going from left to right, of .0504 and .818, respectively. The final estimate of the intervention parameter was also significant and equal to -11.46, respectively. (This final model also included a significant intervention pulse at $t = 105$. This parameter was added to improve the fit of the model, since the strike also affected quarter 105, although to a lesser extent.) Finally, the residuals were white noise.

Table 4-4 gives the ACs and PCs for the Maytag series. Note that these data indicate a possible ARIMA $(0,0,1) \times (0,0,1)_4$ model. However, as shown in Table 4-5, a need for a difference appears in the estimated noise series after simultaneously estimating two intervention parameters (as single pulses) with a fourth-order autoregressive noise model. Once again, this "adjusted" series is quite different from the original series. From this pattern, a number of alternative noise models (or models for the adjusted series) might be identified. We found a $(0,0,0) \times (0,1,1)_4$ with a constant to be adequate (where the difference was on the earnings series).

TABLE 4-5

Maytag Series: Sample Statistics for Noise Series Using High-Order Noise Model Approximation

Lag	Autocorrelation		Partial Autocorrelation	
	Coefficient	Standard Error	Coefficient	Standard Error
1	.7451	.1443	.7451	.1459
2	.5370	.2097	−.0407	.1474
3	.6450	.2366	.5830	.1491
4	.7247	.2708	.1348	.1508
5	.5251	.3085	−.2703	.1525
6	.3950	.3266	.0210	.1543
7	.4663	.3364	−.0335	.1562
8	.5259	.3496	.1589	.1581
9	.3641	.3657	−.1802	.1601
10	.2494	.3732	−.0015	.1622
11	.3041	.3767	−.0406	.1644
12	.3104	.3818	−.1081	.1667

Summary

Previous researchers studying accounting time-series have tended to ignore the effects of interventions on the time-series properties of their data. In this chapter we have discussed two example series where exogenous events have a considerable impact. In addition, we have discussed a technique for identification of a model for the noise series (defined to be the original series "adjusted" for the impact of some intervening event) which utilizes all of the data. Future researchers might consider applying our technique to complete research studies relating to the impact of various events on the time-series properties of various accounting and accounting-related variables.

CHAPTER FIVE

The Impact of the Inclusion of Constant and/or Differencing Factors in the ARIMA Model

As discussed in Chapter One, recent research has indicated that the time-series properties of quarterly EPS can be usefully described by several models, including those studied by Brown and Rozeff [1979], Griffin [1977], and Watts [1975]. In addition, some of these authors have applied the Box-Jenkins modeling process. These models have been studied further by Lorek [1979] and Collins and Hopwood [1980], who investigated their relative ability to predict annual EPS from quarterly EPS. The findings indicate that the forecasts from the individually identified BJ models are reasonably competitive but not more accurate. Therefore, since the BJ modeling process is very time consuming, it has thus far not proven its worth in this type of forecasting.

The previous research, however, has not included a systematic study of the relative accuracy of these models in terms of the choice of differencing and trend. The purpose of the present chapter is to make such an investigation. We choose to study these variables since, as argued in Chatfield and Prothero [1973, p. 33], they will fundamentally affect the shape of the forecasting function. Models without differencing presume a stationary and mean-reverting process; models with differencing and no constant have no fixed mean and presume processes that wander; and models with differencing and a constant assume that the process drifts in a deterministic fashion [Nelson, 1973, p. 63].

Model Estimation

The BR, F, GW, and BJ models were estimated for all of our 267 firms. (See Chapter Two for selection criteria.) The years 1974 through 1978 were used as hold-out periods in order to assess forecast accuracy. Therefore, the 267 firms were each modeled 16 times, once for each method using pre-1974 data (48 quarters in the base period) and again for each method (49 quarters in the base period) using all data prior to the second quarter of 1974, etc. (The BJ models were reidentified each quarter.) The result was that each model made predictions for up to 16 quarters into the future (thus providing a forecast horizon up to 16 quarters) for each of the 16 base periods. For each period in the forecast horizon and each method, the mean absolute relative forecast error was computed.[1]

Empirical Findings

Figure 5-1 presents the forecast error profiles for the BR, F, and GW models. All three profiles are relative to the BJ model, and in each case the forecast error is equal to the

---

[1] The mean absolute relative error is computed as the average of $\left| \frac{\text{Actual EPS-Predicted EPS}}{\text{Actual EPS}} \right|$

Since this error metric can be explosive when the denominator approaches zero, we truncated errors in excess of ten to a value of ten. This operation was required only for a very small percentage of the cases.

TABLE 5-1

Number of Observations Used to Generate Profiles in Figures 5-1 through 5-4

Horizon	PROFILE All Series	 Same as BR and F	 Same as GW
1	5340	335	90
2	5075	322	85
3	4806	310	77
4	4539	295	73
5	4272	278	66
6	4005	262	62
7	3738	252	55
8	3471	243	50
9	3204	231	47
10	2937	214	45
11	2670	196	42
12	2403	180	39
13	2136	162	33
14	1869	141	27
15	1602	119	23
16	1335	97	17

error for the given model minus the BJ error. Therefore, the area below the dotted zero line indicates that the given model error is smaller than the BJ error. Finally, the numbers of observations used to generate Figure 5-1 (as well as Figures 5-2, 5-3, and 5-4) are given in Table 5-1. Note in Figure 5-1 that for forecast horizons up to four quarters, the BR forecasts are more accurate than those of BJ three out of the four times (i.e., the BR line falls below the zero line three out of four times). This superior performance is consistent with the earlier research which indicated that the expensive BJ modeling process is not warranted for a short-term forecasting objective. Note, however, that beyond four quarters all three models dramatically deteriorate relative to the BJ. The upward-sloping lines indicate that the longer the forecast horizon, the greater the deterioration. This phenomenon is particularly interesting since previous research (e.g., Collins and Hopwood [1980]) has made unconditional inferences in terms of one model versus another. These results clearly show that beyond four quarters in the future the BJ provides the most accurate forecasts.

In order to explain this finding, we first consider some background on the BR, F, and GW models relative to the BJ type model. The distinguishing factor of the BJ model is that the BJ modeling process selects a model for *each firm*, whereas the BR, F,and GW models are *single* (or "premier") *models* used for all firms. Early time-series studies used a separate BJ model for each firm. This was because the BJ process attempts to model explicitly all nonrandomness in the data, while the premier models often result in highly correlated residual errors for particular firms. Later, Foster [1977, p. 6] proposed that selecting a separate model for each firm might result in a problem he termed "search bias. That is, sampling variation in a finite sample may lead to the tentative identification

FIGURE 5-1

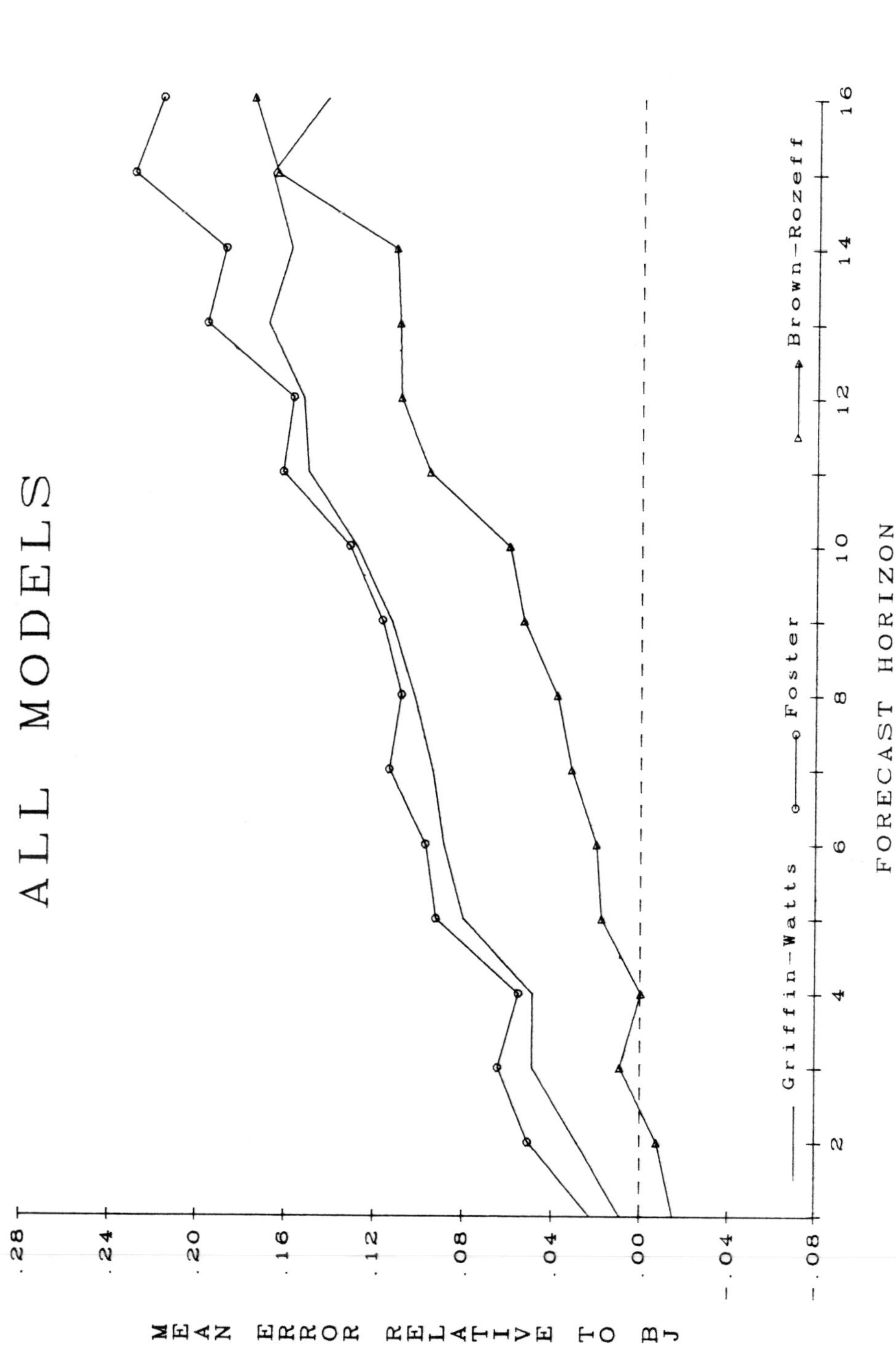
ALL MODELS
MEAN ERROR RELATIVE TO BJ
.28
.24
.20
.16
.12
.08
.04
.00
-.04
-.08
2
4
6
8
10
12
14
16
FORECAST HORIZON
Griffin-Watts
Foster
Brown-Rozeff

FIGURE 5-2

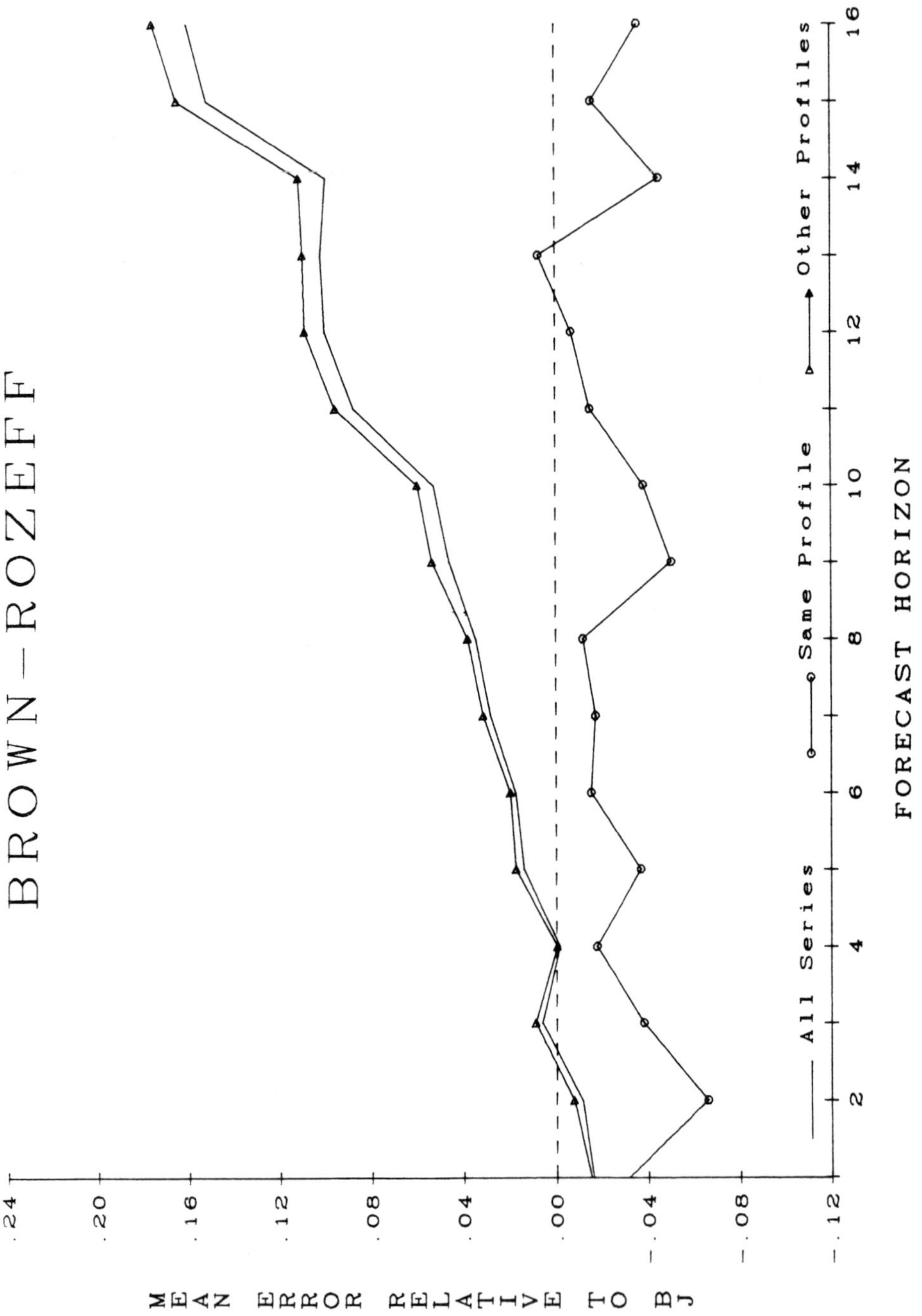
BROWN — ROZEFF
MEAN ERROR RELATIVE TO BJ
.24
.20
.16
.12
.08
.04
.00
-.04
-.08
-.12
2
4
6
8
10
12
14
16
FORECAST HORIZON
All Series
Same Profile
Other Profiles

of a model which is not representative of the underlying time-series." In other words, BJ models may end up including parameters which remove statistically significant, but spurious, residual autocorrelations. (Spurious correlations are those correlations that would appear by chance.) As discussed in Chapter One, subsequent research supported this hypothesis, and BJ model forecasts were not found to be more accurate than those of the single models.

This raises the question: Why then should the BJ models perform better as the forecast horizon increases? Our hypothesis is that while the BJ process is subject to search bias, it does a better job of determining the need for differencing and having a constant term in the model. We consider these factors important because they determine the shape of the forecast function as it converges. Under this hypothesis we would expect the premier models to be at their worst (relative to the BJ) when they disagree with the BJ with respect to the type of differencing and presence of a constant term in the model. Henceforth, we shall say that the premier model has the same *profile* as the BJ when it has the same type of differencing and agrees with the BJ with respect to the need for a constant in the model.[2]

Figures 5-2, 5-3, and 5-4 present evidence on this hypothesis for the BR, F, and GW models. In each case, the firms are partitioned into three groups: 1) all firms (This is the same as Figure 5-1.); 2) those firms where the given premier model has the same profile as the BJ model (In these cases, our hypothesis predicts that the single model should be at its best relative to the BJ.); 3) those firms where the given premier model has a profile which differs from that of the BJ. (In these cases, we would expect the single model to be at its worst.)

Again, these figures show the mean absolute relative error of the premier model minus the same error for the BJ. This means that the lower the line, the more accurate the forecasts are, and a line below the zero line (dotted line) indicates that the premier model outperforms the BJ. Note that for all three premier models, the hypothesis is confirmed. In fact, the BR and GW models actually outperform the BJ models which have the same profile. The Foster model also strongly indicates results in the direction predicted by the hypothesis.

Summary

This chapter investigated the relative ability of several forecast methods proposed in the literature to predict quarterly EPS in terms of the length of the forecast horizon and the presence of differencing and constant terms in the model. It found, contrary to previous notions of "search bias," that (individually identified) Box-Jenkins models provide the most accurate forecasts for forecast horizons more than one year in the future. This phenomenon was empirically consistent with the hypothesis that the single models sometimes use incorrect differencing or omit a constant term from the model, and in those cases where the BJ differs on these factors, it provides the more accurate forecast. In cases where the BJ does not differ on these factors (especially for the BR and GW

---

[2] This is similar to what Dharan [1983b] defines as "model class." He defines models to be in the same model class if they have the same differencing factors.

FIGURE 5-3

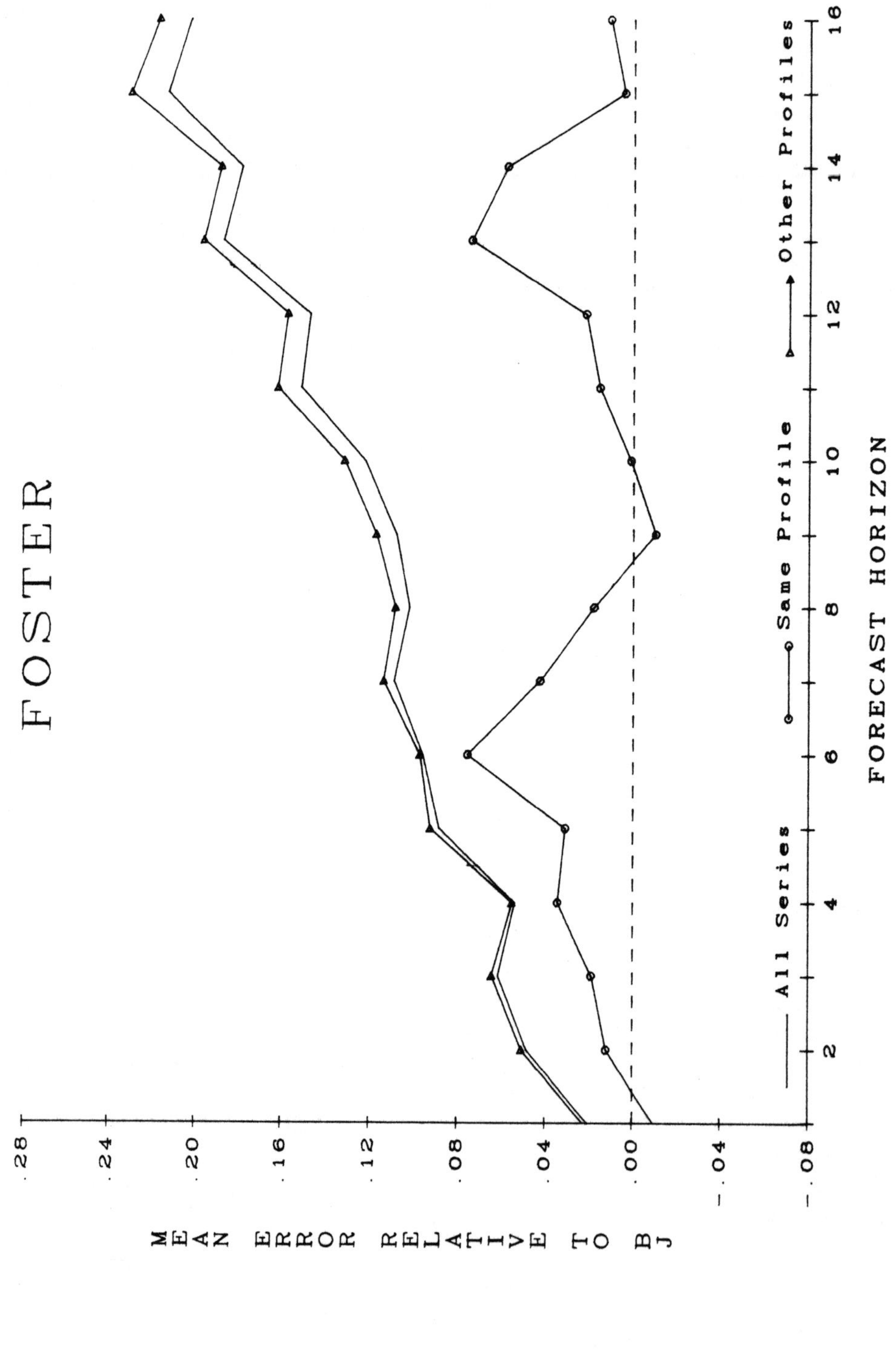
FOSTER
MEAN ERROR RELATIVE TO BJ
.28
.24
.20
.16
.12
.08
.04
.00
-.04
-.08
2
4
6
8
10
12
14
16
FORECAST HORIZON
All Series
Same Profile
Other Profiles

FIGURE 5-4

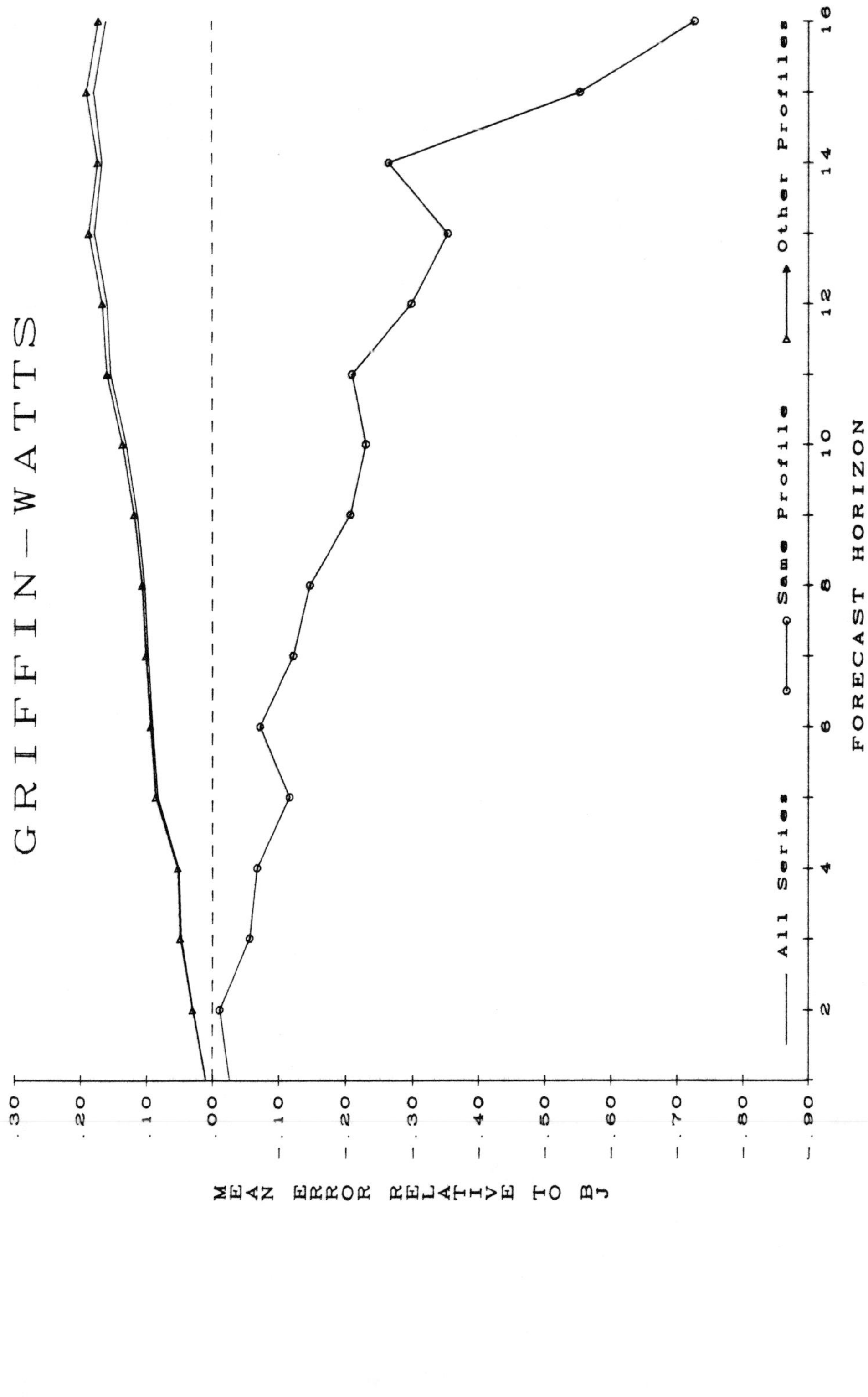
GRIFFIN — WATTS
MEAN ERROR RELATIVE TO BJ
.30
.20
.10
.00
-.10
-.20
-.30
-.40
-.50
-.60
-.70
-.80
-.90
FORECAST HORIZON
2
4
6
8
10
12
14
16
All Series
Same Profile
Other Profiles

models), the premier model gives lower average forecast errors. These results are consistent with the proposition that search bias in individual identification affects selection of the autoregressive and moving-average factors rather than the differencing and constant factors.

The major implication of our findings for empirical analysis is that, while the premier approach may be a useful tool for a large number of heterogeneous firms, it is not true that *all* firms follow the premier process. This should be particularly critical for studies using a small number of firms, studies using forecasts more than one year in the future, or studies where time-series properties themselves are important.

Finally, the present research employs only two factors in partitioning the sample. Other factors also might be used, such as prior predictive ability or best fit within some limited class of models (e.g., the BR, F, and GW models).

CHAPTER SIX

Empirical Evidence on the Potential Private Value of Earnings Forecasts as a Function of the Length of the Forecast Horizon

The Securities and Exchange Commission (SEC) has taken the position that market forces alone are insufficient to cause all material information to be disclosed.[1] In the past, this has led the SEC to favor the concept of urging and/or requiring the disclosure of earnings forecasts. One reason for this is that managements' earnings forecasts have information content [Penman, 1980] which remains "inside information" unless disclosed. This leads to the possibility of trading based on insider information due to differential information dissemination via "black market forecasts."[2] (Henceforth, we refer to this as the "private value argument.") Also, it might be argued that, without required disclosure, useful information might not be available to the market at all.

From a policy-making standpoint, one important issue that arises is the length of the relevant forecast horizon. That is, given that earnings forecasts are to be urged or required, how many quarters into the future should be reported? For example, the SEC has been considering "safe harbor" rules which would, under certain conditions, protect the disclosing company from legal liability associated with errors in forecasting. Should these rules, if adopted, provide protection for forecasts made two quarters into the future—six quarters into the future, etc.? Given the "private value reasoning" of the SEC, this prompts the related question: Is there any private value of forecasts made at, for example, two or six quarters into the future?

The purpose of this chapter is to provide empirical evidence pertinent to the latter question. In particular, this study deals with the problem of assessing the private value of present knowledge of future quarterly earnings.[3] *In an efficient market, this provides an expected upper bound on the value of forecasted earnings from a given time-series model, since the very best that a forecast can do is provide exact present knowledge about a future quarterly earnings number.*

Other related factors also motivate this study. There has been a wide range of research relating to forecasted future earnings. These studies have been involved with dividend policy, association of alternative earnings measures, cost of capital, and management smoothing of earnings.[4] In addition, the accounting information/capital markets re-

---

[1] See Gonedes, Dopuch, and Penman [1976] and Penman [1980] for a more detailed discussion and references.

[2] Gonedes, Dopuch, and Penman [1976, p. 92] concluded that this is one of the SEC's primary reasons for interest in forecast disclosure rules.

[3] By private value we mean the value to an individual, in terms of abnormal return which could be earned, resulting from advance knowledge of earnings. For example, Ball and Brown [1968] found that advance knowledge of the annual income could enable an investor to earn a seven percent abnormal return. As stated in note 2, this type of value has been stated to be a main factor in the SEC's interest in forecast disclosure rules.

[4] See Foster [1977] for references.

search studies typically rely on earnings expectations models (e.g., May [1971], Beaver and Dukes [1972], Brown and Kennelly [1972], Kiger [1972], and Joy, et al. [1977]).

The research relating to forecasted earnings has led to studies which have focused on evaluating various time-series models of quarterly earnings (e.g., Brown and Rozeff [1979], Collins and Hopwood [1980], Foster [1977], Griffin [1977], and Lorek [1979]). Most of these studies have evaluated models based on their ability to predict earnings for some given set of time horizons. Moreover, they have differed widely on the length of time horizon examined. For example, Foster [1977] considered one-quarter-ahead forecasts; Brown and Rozeff [1978] looked at a horizon ranging from one to five quarters; and Brown and Rozeff [1979] reported forecasts for one, five, and nine quarters in the future. Others [Collins and Hopwood, 1980, and Lorek, 1979] focused on the ability of various models to predict annual earnings from quarterly earnings models. The latter studies used a variable time horizon ranging from one to four quarters in the future. (The annual forecasts were formed at each interim period using the known cumulative year-to-date income plus forecasts for the remaining quarters of the year.)

In summary, previous research has varied widely on the choice of the forecast horizon length. There are, however, certain potential problems associated with the selection of an inappropriate horizon length. One such problem can arise if a time horizon investigated is too short. This is because forecast functions for ARIMA models vary in their behavior as the forecast horizon increases (for a more complete discussion, see Box and Jenkins [Chapter 5, 1976] and Chapter Five of the current study). For example, the model $y_t = \phi y_{t-1} + \delta$ has a forecast function $\hat{y}_{t+\ell} = (\phi^{\ell} y_t) + (\phi^{\ell-1}\delta + \phi^{\ell-2}\delta + \cdots + \phi\delta + \delta)$, where y_t is the time-series variable at time t, $\{\phi, \delta\}$ is the set of model parameters, and $\hat{y}_{t+\ell}$ is the forecast for ℓ periods into the future. Note that this forecast is composed of two terms. One depends on the last known value of the series, and the other depends only on the parameter set and ℓ. Therefore, as ℓ is increased, the forecasts depend less upon y_t and more on the series mean.[5] As ℓ approaches infinity, the first term approaches zero and the second term approaches $\frac{\delta}{1-\phi}$, which is the mean of the series (see Nelson [1973, p. 63]). The implication is that different models can have forecast functions which can vary in their relative ability to forecast at differing time horizons. It is, therefore, important that research be conducted to provide a basis for selecting appropriate forecast horizons within a given research context. In the present chapter, this context is taken to be the "private value" framework as set forth by the SEC.

A second difficulty of not knowing the relevant time horizon is that using too long a horizon can result in a loss of data valuable for purposes of assessing forecast accuracy. This is because data retained for holdout periods are not usable for estimation of the model parameters. Therefore, studies using long time horizons may have less data available for model estimation. This can particularly be a problem when sample restrictions cause firms to be excluded due to an insufficient number of data points.

The chapter consists of three parts. Part one discusses the methodology; part two presents empirical results; and part three gives summary and conclusions.

[5]Note also that in the absence of a trend parameter, the second term in the forecast function disappears.

Methodology

Method of Assessing the Information Content of Future Income

As discussed above, *the private value of advance knowledge of future earnings is an expected upper bound on the private value of a given forecast since the forecast at best equals the actual income. Therefore, we evaluate the information content of known future earnings since such information content is necessary for a forecast to be of private value*. This is a simple extension of the Ball and Brown [1968] methodology. They concluded that advance knowledge (i.e., a perfect forecast) of the present year's income would enable an individual to earn a seven percent abnormal return within the present year. We extend this methodology (in a quarterly income context) to consider the value of knowing future quarterly income for various numbers of quarters into the future.

In precise terms, we assess the relationship between $(CAR_t, u_{t,\ell})$ where $u_{t,\ell}$, is the unexpected earnings for ℓ quarters in the future relative to time t, and CAR_t is the cumulative abnormal return for a one-quarter holding period beginning at time t. The computation of these numbers is described below.

Population Studied

Data pertaining to our population of 267 calendar-year firms (described in Chapter One) were obtained from the COMPUSTAT quarterly and CRSP daily tapes. A firm was retained in the population only if it had no missing primary EPS data for the 68 consecutive quarters beginning with the first quarter of 1962 and no missing weekly (Tuesday to Tuesday) returns data for the period from the fourth quarter of 1972 through the fourth quarter of 1978. This provided 12 holdout periods (as defined below) in the inclusive interval containing 1974 through 1978.[6] The EPS number used was primary EPS excluding extraordinary items and discontinued operations, adjusted for capital changes. The return figure selected from CRSP included both dividend and price change components.

Note that, unlike in previous research, *all* firms which met the survivorship test were retained for analysis. We define this group to be the population of interest and make no attempt to generalize to a larger number of years or group of firms.

Abnormal Returns

The market model of the form:

$$(1) \qquad E[\log(1 + \tilde{R}_{it})] = \alpha_i + B_i \log(1 + \tilde{R}_{mt})$$

was estimated, where (1) is the log form of the market model (see Foster [1978]) and R_{it}

---

[6] Although a total of 267 firms was available, the actual number of firms included in the analysis for each holdout period was less than 267 due to missing earnings announcement dates. Each firm in the population was included in the analysis for all holdout periods for which the firm's earnings announcement dates were available.

represents the return for the firm i in period t, R_{mt} represents the value-weighted average market return in period t, and α_i and B_i are model parameters. The estimation was done for each of the 12 holdout periods using ordinary least squares regression. This was accomplished in each case by including weekly data for the 65 weeks preceding the week containing the first market day of the quarter. This procedure was repeated for 12 consecutive quarters with the regression for the first quarter containing data for the 65 weeks prior to the week containing the first market day of 1974. The residuals from these models, when applied to the holding periods (the inclusive interval from the week containing the first market day of the quarter to the week containing the announcement date), constitute risk-adjusted abnormal returns. These abnormal returns were then individually summed across each holding period to give each firm's cumulative abnormal return (CAR_t) for the holding period t, = 1, ..., 12.

Earnings Expectation Models

Unexpected income numbers were generated by subtracting from actual income a time-series forecast. Several time-series models were used. These included those used by Brown and Rozeff [1979], Griffin [1977], and Watts [1975]. Also, a full Box-Jenkins (individual identification) analysis was conducted for each firm for each holdout period. These models were discussed in Chapter One, as well as elsewhere (see Collins and Hopwood [1980] and Lorek [1979]). All of these models provided the same results relative to the research question in this chapter.

The model parameters corresponding to each of the 12 holdout periods described above were estimated. Therefore, the first estimation included all earnings data prior to the first quarter of 1974; the second estimation included all earnings data prior to the second quarter of 1974, etc. For the Box-Jenkins analysis, the models were both reidentified and reestimated each quarter.

Next, each of the 12 models was used to generate forecasts from one to eight quarters into the future. For example, the first model, estimated with data prior to 1974, made forecasts for the first quarter of 1974 through the fourth quarter of 1975. Similarly, the second model, estimated with data prior to the first quarter of 1974, made forecasts for the second quarter of 1974 through the first quarter of 1976, etc. An eight-quarter-ahead time horizon was used in order to include at least two seasonal periods.

Let the unexpected income ($u_{t,\ell}$) be defined as $A_{t+\ell} - F_{t,\ell}$, where A denotes the actual income and F denotes forecasted income, t identifies the holding period, and forecast lead time ℓ refers to the number of quarters in the future relative to the beginning of the holding period. By this definition, $u_{t,1}$ (i.e., $\ell = 1$) refers to the unexpected income for holding period t(t = 1, ..., 12). Note that previous research (e.g., Brown and Kennelly [1972]) focused on this contemporaneous association between CAR_t and $u_{t,1}$. Our generalization of this research involves measuring the association between CAR_t and $u_{t,\ell}$ for $\ell > 1$ as well as $\ell = 1$. To the degree that such an association exists, it would be possible to earn an abnormal return *in the present holding period* based upon advance knowledge (a perfect forecast) of income at period $t + \ell$.

Note that this same approach could be used for other definitions of a holding period. For example, instead of our one-quarter holding period, it would be possible to use a two-quarter definition. We chose the one-quarter definition because it is the minimum reporting interval generally used by companies. Using a longer period would involve aggregation of the quarterly numbers and a corresponding potential information loss. For example, if the benefit of advance knowledge was limited to one-quarter-ahead earnings, then the relative advantage of the one-quarter-ahead information would be diluted in the aggregation required to use a two-quarter holding period.

Finally, Figure 6-1 summarizes the procedures used to compute CAR_t and $u_{t,\ell}$. Each vertical bar represents the end of a quarter. Note that the figure is divided into three main components which include the estimation period, the holding period, and the forecast horizon.

Empirical Results

Early studies, such as Ball and Brown [1968], measured the information content of earnings based upon an investment strategy which involved long sales for a positive unexpected income and short sales for a negative unexpected income. Others, such as Foster [1977], have used this same technique by using a two-by-two contingency table to test for association between abnormal return and unexpected income. More recent research, however, has noted that this approach ignores the magnitude of the data. It has been demonstrated both empirically [Beaver, Clark, and Wright, 1979] and theoretically [Ohlson, 1979] that the association can be more comprehensively measured via the correlation (or rank correlation) coefficient. This, of course, presumes that the relation between unexpected income and CAR can be described by a simple linear model. This assumption seems reasonably justified from our analysis of the findings of Beaver, Clark, and Wright [1979]. In addition, as discussed below, we analyzed our data with respect to this assumption.

Since different firms and income numbers are of different scale, unexpected income was defined as $\frac{A-F}{|F|}$ where A is the actual and F is the forecasted income.[7] Since this number is subject to near-zero denominators (and therefore explosive realizations), we considered the rank of this number across the firms. On the other hand, for the results presented, we did not rank the CAR values since the reasons for ranking did not exist there.[8]

Given our ranking procedure we computed, for each holding period t, the signed squared correlation (henceforth referred to as simply correlation) between CAR_t and $u_{t,\ell}$, $\ell = 1, \cdots, 8$, $t = 1, \cdots, 12$. Use of the signed squared correlations as opposed to the squared correlations mitigates the problem of averaging in negative

[7] We use the forecasted number as the denominator to measure the surprise value associated with the forecast error. Therefore, our measure was based on the expectation instead of the actual number.

[8] To assess the appropriateness of using a linear model to describe the relationship between CAR and u_t, we analyzed the residuals from the above described regression models. Statistical tests of skew and kurtosis did not indicate departure from normality. In addition, histograms indicated the distribution to be symmetric and bell-shaped. Finally, we redid the entire analysis treating CAR as a ranked variable, without any change in results.

Figure 6-1

Explanation of Procedures Used to Compute CAR_t and Unexpected Earnings $u_{t,\ell}$

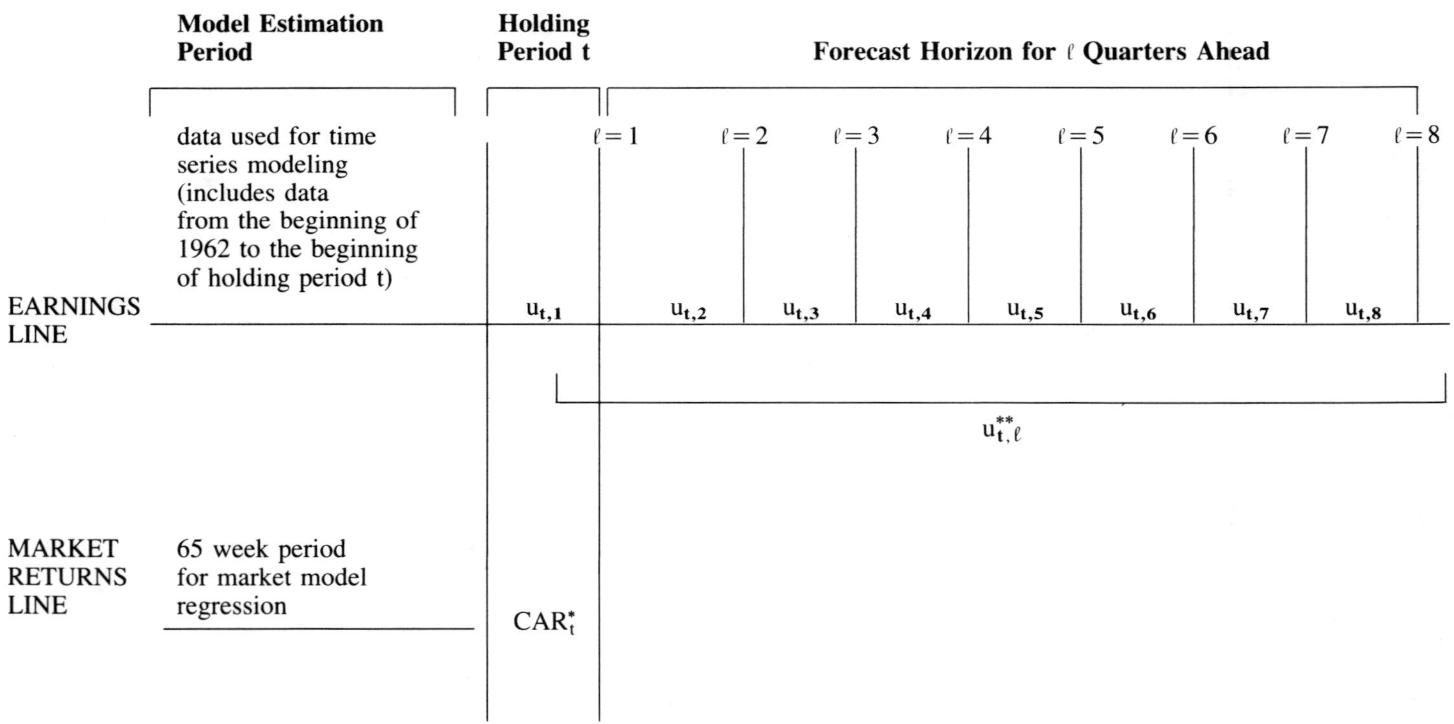

* Computed by using model on prior 65 week period to compute residuals using data during holding period t

** $u_{t,\ell}$ is the unexpected earnings (forecast error) for holding period t and lead time ℓ ($\ell = 1, 2, \ldots, 8$)

TABLE 6-1

Correlation Between CAR and Rank of Unexpected Earnings as a Function of Forecast Horizon Length

Horizon Length*	Signed R^2		
	BR	GW	BJ
1	.0426	.0577	.0480
2	.0542	.0605	.0697
3	.0511	.0481	.0495
4	.0286	.0359	.0129
5	.0293	.0321	.0243
6	.0396	.0379	.0487
7	.0148	.0311	.0361
8	.0187	.0242	.0167

*Number of quarters in the future relative to the beginning of period t.

correlations as positive numbers. Table 6-1 presents these correlations averaged across the 12 holding periods.[9,10] The results are surprising in that a consistent pattern of correlations persists for the entire set of time horizons. This, however, should not be interpreted to mean that the advance knowledge of income at longer horizons contains *incremental* information content. To assess this incremental content of advance knowledge of earnings as a function of horizon length, we considered the partial correlation between CAR_t and the ranked $u_{t,\ell}$ with $u_{t,\ell-1}$, $u_{t,\ell-2}$, • • •, u_{t-1} held constant. The results of this analysis are presented in Table 6-2. Here, the first correlation (COR) is $COR(CAR_t, u_{t,1})$ which is the same as the first correlation in Table 1. The second correlation is $COR\ (CAR_t,\ u_{t,\ 2}|u_{t,1})$; the third correlation is $COR\ (CAR_t,\ u_{t,3}|u_{t,1}, u_{t,2})$, etc. To interpret the meaning of these numbers, consider a linear regression between the dependent variable CAR and independent variables $u_{t,1}$, $u_{t,2}$, • • •, $u_{t,\ell-1}$. Then the numbers in Table 6-2 describe the proportional reduction in the unexplained variation in CAR_t by adding $u_{t,\ell}$ to this linear regression model. This marginal explanation gives a measure of how much better one can predict CAR_t given advance knowledge of an additional quarter's income.

Note that Table 6-2 shows that the incremental value of a perfect forecast, as a function of lead time, dampens out very rapidly. Beyond three quarters ahead, the association is practically zero. These data indicate little private value in having perfect forecasts of the quarterly income for time horizons four or more quarters in the future. Note that the probable reason for the rapid dampening of the value of private information is that the

[9] Our analysis of the data indicated that the results were consistent for all four of the years' quarterly reporting periods. Therefore, averaging across holding periods did not result in a loss of information.

[10] When evaluating the size of the first signed squared correlation relative to other results, recall that this result is for individual firms rather than portfolios. Also, the signed squared measurement is conservative.

TABLE 6-2

Partial Correlation Between CAR and Unexpected Earnings as a Function of Forecast Horizon

Horizon Length*	Signed Partial R^2		
	BR	GW	BJ
1	.0426	.0579	.0461
2	.0288	.0195	.0253
3	.0108	.0022	.0090
4	.0013	-.0009	-.0035
5	-.0027	-.0009	-.0013
6	.0019	.0023	-.0004
7	.0004	.0013	-.0035
8	-.0041	.0023	-.0059

*Number of quarters in the future relative to the beginning of period t.

market probably does not have very accurate expectations of earnings per share more than two or three quarters ahead. Therefore, the investor who has the private information concerning long-horizon future earnings numbers receives little present benefit from his knowledge because other investors do not acquire the information during the holding period. (For example, he knows that a stock is "good" but no one else does; the price of that stock stays constant, and he gets no benefit from his knowledge.) Obviously, if this scenario is correct, an improvement in the accuracy of long-horizon market expectations of earnings per share would increase the length of the horizon which would yield private value. It should be emphasized that the dampening of private value reported above does not mean that an investor would not want to know the income four or more quarters ahead, but rather that this information cannot be used to advantage in the *present* holding period. Such information could always be used advantageously in a later holding period, as long as the holding period is sufficiently close to the quarter to which the forecast relates.

Summary

This chapter has considered the problem of determining the potential private value of forecasts of future quarterly earnings. Analysis of the data indicated that the addition of perfect knowledge of quarterly earnings for periods more than three quarters in the future (given knowledge of earnings one through three quarters in the future) would not enable an individual to earn an abnormal return within the current one-quarter holding period.

From a policy-making point of view, the interpretation is somewhat more complex. It must first be said that the results are consistent with the hypothesis that there is no incremental present-period private value to having knowledge of four (or more)-quarter-ahead earnings. This does not necessarily mean that there would be no social value to such knowledge.[11] On the other hand, the results are consistent with the reasoning that the decision to require disclosure of earnings forecasts for four (or more) quarters ahead should not be made on the basis of preventing some individuals from having an advantage due to ‘‘inside’’ access (as considered by the SEC) to this information—at least as long as this information is in the form of a forecast and the intervening three quarters' forecasts are available.

The implications of the results for research on the time-series of earnings are that studies concerned with private value of information should focus on performance within the very short run and should be less concerned with forecasts at long horizons, such as nine quarters ahead used in one study cited above. In addition, these studies should consider a time horizon of at least three quarters into the future. Note that *these results apply only under the current information set*. If, for example, the SEC were to require management forecasts for the three-quarter-ahead horizon, the private value results would probably change.

[11] For example, forecasts for two years in the future might be used by economic planners in the projection of GNP.

CHAPTER SEVEN

Summary and Conclusions

The research findings in the previous chapters dealt with five issues relating to univariate time-series analysis of interim earnings. Our findings relating to each of these are summarized below.

Stationarity and Invertibility Problems

We found the estimation of noninvertible or nonstationary parameters to be a common problem. As expected, use of models with these parameters resulted in deterioration in forecast accuracy. We presented a technique of constrained estimation that was found to be simple to implement and useful in solving the problem.

Our principal result implies that researchers should consider using constrained estimation, particularly in small-sample situations where one or two series could have forecast errors that dominate the average forecast error for the sample.

Residual Distributions and Power Transformations

Analysis of model residuals for skewness and kurtosis indicated a marked problem with kurtotic sample distributions. In addition, the average ratio of the variance of the second half of the residual series relative to the variance of the first half of the residual series was eight or more. Both of these problems point to severe violations of the assumptions required for maximum likelihood estimation of model parameters. It was found that application of the Box-Cox transformation greatly mitigated but did not eliminate this problem. The residuals of models using the transformation appeared, on the average, to be free of skew and kurtosis problems. On the other hand, the variance ratio was reduced to two times as opposed to eight-plus times, but this is still inconsistent with model assumptions. Consistent with this finding, forecast errors were not reduced for models containing a transformation parameter as compared to models using untransformed data.

Future research on this problem might consider several directions. One might be to consider use of a more general nonlinear time-series model. Another approach might be to use a Kalman filter approach, since this approach does not require a constant variance over time. This could even be explored in conjunction with use of the Box-Cox transformation. Finally, various economic transformations might be considered, such as a general price-level adjustment. It is reasonable to expect that a large amount of the increasing variance problem is due to higher levels of prices over time.

Estimation of Intervention Model Without Dividing the Sample

A technique for intervention analysis was explored that allows the use of the entire time-series including an observation for which an intervening event occurs. The procedure involves conducting the normal model identification on an ''adjusted series,'' a series from which the impact of the outlier has been removed by a simple ordinary least-squares technique. In the cases studied, it was found that use of the unadjusted series would result in the wrong model identification, and the identification process was considerably enhanced by using the ''adjusted'' series. Future research in this area might consider the application of our method to more complicated situations such as changes in inventory methods.

The Impact of the Choice of Differencing and Trend

As discussed in Chapter One, previous research has shown that using a single model for all series produces forecast errors no larger, on the average, than those associated with full Box-Jenkins (individual identification) analysis. The hypothesis was set forth that for some series, this result might not hold because the single model approach is inflexible with regard to the type of differencing used and the choice as to whether or not to include a constant in the model. The data confirmed this hypothesis. It was found that when the individually identified model differed from the single model (in terms of differencing and constant), the individually identified model, on the average, produced a smaller forecast error. On the other hand, the individually identified model produced an equal or larger average error for cases where it did not differ from the single model in terms of differencing and trend. An additional finding was that the individually identified model produced the most accurate forecasts for forecast horizons greater than one year in the future.

Private Value of Earnings Forecasts

Our data indicated that there was no private value (abnormal return during the next quarter) from increasing the horizon of advance (private) knowledge of quarterly earnings beyond three quarters into the future. We found the ''window of opportunity'' to be limited to a maximum of three quarters prior to the announcement date. For example, given private advance knowledge of an interim earnings number one hundred years in the future, one would basically have to wait approximately 99 ¼ years to benefit from this information.

The implication of our result for others relates to our expectation that the private value of advance knowledge of the actual earnings number should be an upper bound on the value of advance knowledge of a forecast for the same time horizon, since a forecast at best equals the actual earnings number. Therefore, given our results, it would seem that it would be useful to place our emphasis on short-run forecasting, especially when a limited amount of data is available. We acknowledge, however, that there may be other considerations that affect the length of the horizon studied. One such example is budgeting. Surely, companies are interested in forecasting their profits one year or more in advance.

Conclusion

The results of our study indicate that now might be the appropriate time for researchers to pay more attention to some of the "finer details" of modeling earnings (and other) time-series. Specifically, more attention might be given to the distributional and estimation issues (via transformation and constrained estimation) as well as model identification issues. In addition, it might be useful to explore the use of intervention analysis in more detail, since history tells us that accounting series are full of interventions such as strikes, accounting changes, etc. Finally, our private value results in Chapter Six should provide some guidance for focusing on an appropriate forecast horizon for study.

Research in accounting time-series analysis is undoubtedly moving from a univariate to a multivariate framework. Such research will involve a blending of econometrics, economic theory, and time-series model building. This framework will involve processes considerably more complex than in the univariate case. Our feeling is that researchers need to obtain a firm grasp of univariate models before proceeding to multivariate situations.

REFERENCES

Abdel-khalik, A. R. and R. B. Thompson, "Research on Earnings Forecasts: The State of the Art," *The Accounting Journal* (Winter 1977-78), pp. 180-209.

Albrecht, W. S. And J. C. McKeown, "Toward an Extended Use of Statistical Analytical Reviews in the Audit," *Proceedings of Auditing Research Symposium*, Center for International Education and Research in Accounting (1977), University of Illinois, pp. 53-69.

Albrecht, W. S., L. L. Lookabill and J. C. McKeown, "The Time Series Properties of Annual Earnings," *Journal of Accounting Research* (Autumn 1977), pp. 226-244.

Ball, Ray and P. Brown, "An Empirical Evaluation of Accounting Income Numbers," *Journal of Accounting Research* (Autumn 1968), pp. 159-178.

Ball, Ray and R. L. Watts, "Some Time Series Properties of Accounting Income Numbers," *Journal of Finance* (June 1972), pp. 663-681.

Bao, D.-h., M. T. Lewis, W. T. Lin, and J. G. Manegold, "Applications of Time-Series Analysis in Accounting: A Review," *Journal of Forecasting* (October-December 1983), pp. 405-423.

Beaver, W. H., "The Time Series Properties of Earnings," *Empirical Research in Accounting: Selected Studies* (Supplement to *Journal of Accounting Research*, 1970), pp. 62-99.

———, R. G. Clarke, and W. F. Wright, "The Association Between Unsystematic Security Returns and Magnitude of Earnings Forecast Errors," *Journal of Accounting Research* (Autumn 1979), pp. 316-340.

Beaver, W. H. and R. E. Dukes, "Interperiod (Naive) Tax Allocation Earnings Expectations and the Behavior of Security Prices," *The Accounting Review* (April 1972), pp. 320-332.

Beaver, W. H., J. W. Kennelly, and W. M. Voss, "Predictive Ability as a Criterion for the Evaluation of Accounting Data," *The Accounting Review* (October 1968), pp. 678-683.

Beaver, W., R. Lambert and D. Morse, "The Information Content of Security Prices," *Journal of Accounting and Economics* (March 1980), pp. 3-28.

Box, G. E. P. and D. R. Cox, "An Analysis of Transformations," *Journal of American Statistical Association* (1964), pp. 70-79.

Box, G. E. P. and G. M. Jenkins, *Time Series Analysis: Forecasting and Control* (Holden-Day, 1976).

Box, G. E. P. and Ljung, *Technical Report #477* (University of Wisconsin Statistics Department, 1976).

Box, G. E. P. and G. C. Tiao, "Intervention Analysis with Applications to Economic and Environmental Problems," *Journal of American Statistical Association* (1975), pp. 70-79.

Brealy, R. A., *Introduction to Risk and Return from Common Stocks* (MIT Press, 1969).

Brown, Philip and J. W. Kennelly, "The Informational Content of Quarterly Earnings: An Extension and Some Further Evidence," *Journal of Business* (July 1972), pp. 403-415.

Brown, L. D. and M. S. Rozeff, "The Superiority of Analyst Forecasts as Measures of Expectations: Evidence From Earnings," *Journal of Finance* (March 1978), pp. 1-16.

———, "Univariate Time Series Models of Quarterly Earnings Per Share Behavior," *Journal of Finance* (Spring 1979), pp. 13-21.

Chant, P. D., "On the Predictability of Corporate Earnings Per Share," *Journal of Finance* (1980), pp. 13-21.

Chatfield, C. and D. L. Prothero, "Box-Jenkins Seasonal Forecasting: Problems in a Case Study," *Journal of Royal Statistical Society* (1973), pp. 295-336.

Coates, R., "The Predictive Content of Interim Reports – A Time Series Analysis," *Journal of Accounting Research* (Supplement, 1972), pp. 132-144.

Collins, W. A. and W. S. Hopwood, "A Multivariate Analysis of Annual Earnings Forecasts Generated from Quarterly Forecasts of Financial Analysts and Univariate Time Series Models," *Journal of Accounting Research* (Fall 1980).

Copeland, R. M. and R. J. Marioni, "Executives' Forecasts of Earnings Per Share Versus Forecasts of Naive Models," *Journal of Business* (October 1972), pp. 497-512.

Cragg, J. G. and B. G. Malkiel, "The Consensus and Accuracy of Some Predictions of the Growth of Corporate Earnings," *Journal of Finance* (Spring 1968), pp. 67-84.

Dharan, B. G., "Identification and Estimation Issues for a Causal Earnings Model," *Journal of Accounting Research* (Spring 1983a), pp. 18-41.

———, "Empirical Identification Procedures for Earnings Models," *Journal of Accounting Research* (Spring 1983b), pp. 256-270.

Dopuch, Nicholas and R. L. Watts, "Using Time Series Models to Assess the Significance of Accounting Changes," *Journal of Accounting Research* (Spring 1972), pp. 180-194.

Fama, E. F., "The Behavior of Stock Market Prices," *Journal of Business* (January 1965), pp. 34-105.

———, "Efficient Capital Markets: A Review of Theory and Empirical Work," *Journal of Finance* (May 1970), pp. 383-417.

Financial Accounting Standards Board, *Tentative Conclusions on Objectives of Financial Statements of Business Enterprises* (FASB, 1976).

———, Statement of Financial Accounting Concepts No. 1: Objectives of Financial Reporting and Elements of Financial Statements of Business Enterprises (FASB, 1978).

Foster, George, "Quarterly Accounting Data: Time Series Properties and Predictive Ability Results," *The Accounting Review* (January 1977), pp. 1-21.

———, *Financial Statement Analysis* (Prentice-Hall, 1978).

Frank, Werner, "A Study of the Predictive Significance of Two Income Measures," *Journal of Accounting Research* (Spring 1969), pp. 123-136.

Gonedes, N. J., N. Dopuch and S. H. Penman, "Disclosure Rules, Information-Production, and Capital Market Equilibrium: The Case for Forecast Disclosure Rules," *Journal of Accounting Research* (Spring 1976), pp. 89-137.

Green, D., "Towards a Theory of Interim Reports," *Journal of Accounting Research* (Spring 1964), pp. 35-49.

——— and J. Segall, "The Predictive Power of First Quarter Earnings Reports," *Journal of Business* (January 1967), pp. 44-55.

Griffin, P. A., "The Time Series Behavior of Quarterly Earnings: Preliminary Evidence," *Journal of Accounting Research* (Spring 1977), pp. 71-83.

Hopwood, W. S. and J. C. McKeown, "An Evaluation of Univariate Time Series Earnings Models and Their Generalization to a Single Input Transfer Function," *Journal of Accounting* (Autumn 1981).

———, and P. Newbold, "Power Transformations in Time Series Models of Quarterly Earnings Per Share," *The Accounting Review* (October 1981), pp. 927-933.

Hopwood, W. S. and P. Newbold, "Time Series Analysis of Accounting: A Survey and Analysis of Recent Issues," *Journal of Time Series Analysis* (October 1981), pp. 135-199.

Jazwinski, A. H., *Stochastic Processes and Filtering Theory* (Academic Press, 1970).

Joy, O. M., R. H. Litzenberger, and R. W. McNally, "The Adjustment of Stock Price to Announcements of Unanticipated Changes in Quarterly Earnings," *Journal of Accounting Research* (1977), pp. 207-225.

Judge, G. G., W. E. Griffiths, R. C. Hill, and T. Lee, *The Theory and Practice of Econometrics* (Wiley, 1980).

Kiger, J. E., "An Empirical Investigation of NYSE Volume and Price Reactions to the Announcement of Quarterly Earnings," *Journal of Accounting Research* (Spring 1972), pp. 113-128.

Kinney, W. R., "ARIMA and Regression in Analytical Review: An Empirical Test," *The Accounting Review* (January 1978), pp. 48-60.

Lintner, J., "The Valuation of Risk Assets and Selection of Risky Investments in Stock Portfolios and Capital Budgets," *Review of Economics and Statistics* (February 1965), pp. 13-27.

Little, I. M. D., *Higgledy, Piggledy Growth* (Oxford University of Statistics, 1962).

——— and A. C. Rayner, *Higgledy, Piggledy Growth Again* (Oxford University of Statistics--Blackwell, 1966).

Lookabill, L. L., "Some Additional Evidence on the Time Series Properties of Accounting Earnings," *The Accounting Review* (February 1976), pp. 724-738.

——— and J. C. McKeown, "Time Series Properties of Stock Market Returns," *AIDS National Convention Proceedings* (1976).

Lorek, L. S., "Predicting Annual Net Earnings with Quarterly Earnings Time-Series Models," *Journal of Accounting Research* (Spring 1979), pp. 190-204.

Luenberger, D. G., *Introduction to Linear and Nonlinear Programming* (Addison-Wesley, 1973).

May, R. G., "The Influence of Quarterly Earnings Announcements on Investor Decisions as Reflected in Common Stock Price Changes," *Supplement to Journal of Accounting Research* (1971), pp. 119-171.

Mossin, J., "Equilibrium in a Capital Market," *Econometrica* (October 1966), pp. 768-783.

Nelson, C. R., *Applied Time Series Analysis for Managerial Forecasting* (Holden-Day, 1973).

Norby, W. C., *Disclosure of Corporate Forecasts to the Inventors* (The Financial Analysts Federation, 1973).

Ohlson, J., "Residual (API) Analysis and the Private Value of Information," *Journal of Accounting Research* (Autumn 1979), pp. 506-527.

Penman, S. H., "An Empirical Investigation of the Voluntary Disclosure of Corporate Earnings Forecasts," *Journal of Accounting Research* (Spring 1980), pp. 132-160.

Praetz, P. D., "Testing for a Flat Spectrum on Efficient Market Price Data," *Journal of Finance* (June 1979), pp. 645-658.

Prakash, P. and A. Rappaport (Eds.), *Public Reporting of Corporate Financial Forecasts* (New York: Commerce Clearing House, 1974).

Reilly, R. K., E. L. Morgensen, and M. West, "The Predictive Ability of Alternative Parts of Interim Financial Statements," *Empirical Research in Accounting: Selected Studies* (Supplement to *Journal of Accounting Research,* 1972), pp. 105-124.

Revsine, L., "Predictive Ability, Market Prices and Operating Flows," *The Accounting Review* (July 1971), pp. 480-489.

Salamon, G. L. and E. D. Smith, "Additional Evidence on the Time Series Properties of Reported Earnings Per Share," *Journal of Finance* (December 1977), pp. 1795-1801.

Sharpe, W. F., "Capital Asset Prices: A Theory of Market Equilibrium Under Condition of Risk," *Journal of Finance* (September 1964), pp. 425-442.

Simmons, J. and J. Gray," An Investigation of the Effect of Differing Accounting Frameworks on the Prediction of Income," *The Accounting Review* (October 1969), pp. 757-776.

Stringer, K. W., "A Statistical Technique for Analytical Review," *Studies on Statistical Methodology in Auditing* (Supplement to *Journal of Accounting Research*, 1975), pp. 1-29.

Wall Street Journal, "SEC Again to Urge Profit Projections Other Operating Forecasts by Companies," (February 1978), p. 6.

Watts, R. L., "The Time Series Behavior of Quarterly Earnings," Department of Commerce, University of Newcastle (1975).

——— and R. L. Leftwich, "The Time Series of Annual Accounting Earnings," *Journal of Accounting Research* (Autumn 1977), pp. 253-271.